GRAMMA LARSO

Jesus,
Her Friend

Enjy
Gram's Poems
Roy Wolf
Helen O. Larson

Helen O. Larson with her husband Ivar are pictured on their wedding day in 1957. Later in life she would be known as Gramma Larson.

On the cover: Gramma Larson sends her love from above and hopes you find her poems inspiring.

GRAMMA LARSON REMEMBERS

Jesus,
Her Friend

Raymond A. Wolf

Featuring Poems by
Helen O. Larson

W O L F
PUBLISHING

Published by Wolf Publishing
Hope, Rhode Island

Printed in the United States of America

For all general information:
E-mail: **theewolf@cox.net**

For orders:

Visit us on the Internet at: **www.raywolfbooks.com**

To
my Mom,
Helen O. Larson,
who has been waiting
patiently for me to publish
her poetry about her friend, Jesus

Contents

Acknowledgments

This sixth book in the *Gramma Larson Remembers* series is in response to many of my customers asking when I was going to publish my mom's religious poems. Therefore, this book is for you.

I am so grateful to Jennifer Carnevale for editing my seventeenth title. Thank you so much.

All images are from the author's collection.

Introduction

Helen O. Larson wrote her first poem at the age of 12 in 1922 and her last poem at the age of 94 in 2005. The following pages contain the ones she wrote about her friend, Jesus.

Chapter One Dates Unknown records all of Gramma's poems about her friend, Jesus that were not dated. I presume they were written before the 1970s. They are all listed alphabetically.

Chapter Two The 1970s seems to be when she started dating her poems. From this chapter on her poems are presented in order by date.

Chapter Three The 1980s she continues dating her poems. They also become more frequent, especially after her husband, Ivar, passed away.

Chapter Four The 1990s finds Gramma living alone except for her friend, Jesus. The frequency is slowing as she is slowing also.

Chapter Four The 2000s escorts Gramma into her 90s. Her writing has slowed considerably. January 2002, finds her in the hospital and then to a nursing home. I did not feel she belonged there and took her home. However, in January 2003 it is back to the hospital and then to the nursing home again. I still did not believe she belonged there and again brought her home. This time she made it to 2005 and yes, I took her home but she only made five days and was back at the nursing home. At this point it was unspoken but we both felt this was it. This is when she gave up and decided to let Jesus take her home to Ivar.

Whenever possible, I have included copies of Gramma's original hand written poems. I previously included some originals in her *Famous People, Family and Friends* book and they were received with overwhelming enthusiasm. People commented to me it was like she was there with them writing the poem as they were reading it.

When Gramma mentions that Jesus healed her, she is referring to the time she had gallstones and was to be operated on. At the last minute the doctor said she must have passed them and canceled the operation.

I will conclude my introduction with the following poem. It expresses her strong desire to spread Jesus' word through her poems.

My Precious Jesus

Jesus every day
I'm watching for you
I want to see your hands
Where the nails went through

In your word I read
How you pardon and forgive
Please forgive me Jesus
For with you I want to live

Someday you'll come back
And take me away
I live and look forward
To that glorious day

Will you be wearing
A robe of sparkling white
I know it will be
Some day or night

Jesus it seems I can feel your holy power
I've seen the miracles you perform
I believe in your holy spirit
Since I've been reborn

Help me tell others
They must come to you
Then they'll live forever
When this life is through

So through my poems I'll tell others how you have set me free
And how you gave forgiveness to a sinner such as me

One

Dates Unknown

United once again for all eternity.

A Kind and Gentle Man

Oh! That kind and gentle man
That lived in the Holy Land across the sea
He mingled with the faithful and sinners too
And He died for you and me

He knew He had lost a little lamb
And He left the flock one day
And went to search for the lamb
Who had strayed away

He preached to the sinners
He told them to repent
And the crowds followed Him
Wherever He went

Though He gave His life
On a cross one day
He still lives in His home in Heaven
So we must always pray

He always hears our prayers
He's compassionate and kind
And my brother and sister
He's the truest friend you'll ever find

Someday when I meet Him
His nail scarred hands I'll see
And then I will thank Him
For laying them on me

Always There

When troubles cause me sorrow
And I don't know what to do
I know I can always
Kneel and pray to you

When my heart is breaking
And no one seems to care
I can always count on you
For you are always there

When sorrows weigh me down
And it seems I can't go on
I know I can depend on you
To keep me safe from harm

Why did you care so much
That you died for me
You were nailed on a cross
Made from a dogwood tree

As I shed so many tears
Satan gets hold of me
He's angry because I'm helping you
Because you died to set me free

An Apparition

It seemed Jesus stood on a mountain
Surrounded by a beautiful light
Oh! What a heavenly vision
In a robe of virgin white

It seemed I heard Him say
My children turn from sin
And if you will ask me
I will take you in

It seemed He said I died
On a rough old tree
I gladly paid the ransom
So you could be free

It seemed He said I'm coming back again
So repent and pray
For God is the only one that knows
That appointed day

It seemed the apparition faded
The stars were out that night
And I will always remember
The vision it seemed I saw that night

Christ's Chapel

As I entered Christ's chapel
On one winter day
Tears rolled from my eyes
As I kneeled to pray

I poured out my heart
As I prayed to Him
I was sobbing and crying
As the organ played a hymn

As the music filled the chapel
And I was kneeling there
I was ever so grateful
Because Christ did care

As I arose to go
And walked down the aisle
I stopped to adore Him
And I tried hard to smile

Later that night at home
By my bed in prayer
I felt so comforted
Just to know He was there

I arose from my bedside
Where I had kneeled to pray
I was so glad I had gone
To Christ's chapel that day

Come Follow Me

A Holy man named Jesus
Lived many years ago
It's true, I know it's true
The Bible tells us so

He was so kind and gentle
He healed the sick and lame
He told about His father in Heaven
And the reason why He came

He was a preacher while He lived there
He was a carpenter too
And if you pray to Him
He will listen to you

He's living my friend
Believe what you cannot see
And you may hear this Jesus
Saying, come follow me

He was a shepherd
He did many things
He sits on a throne in Heaven
He's crowned King of Kings

If you are sad and lonely
Turn your life over to Him
Praise Him each and every day
For He's coming back again

Come Walk With Me

Can't you hear the Savior saying
Take my hand come walk with me
I will lead you down the right road
And from sin I'll set you free

Come walk with me my child
It's the only way
I showed my love for you
When they took my life away

Come walk with me, come walk with me
I'm calling can't you hear
You cannot see my child
But I am always near

Come walk with me, come walk with me
I'm calling from my Heavenly home
Just as you are, I'll accept you
And you'll never be alone

Come walk with me, come walk with me
My human life I had to give
If you'll always walk with me
Eternal life to you I'll give

Every Tear Drop

Lord Jesus you see every tear drop
That falls from my eyes
If you wasn't there to console me
I could never get by

When I walk along life's highway
And no one seems to care
Precious Lord and Savior
You are always there

I like to imagine that
You're behind the clouds each day
That you're looking down
And guiding me along the way

I was so lost and lonely
Until I found you
But I'm happy that I did
For you are a friend so true

When friends desert me
And leave me alone
I can make it through the day
For you're in your Heavenly home

Faithful Friend

Don't turn away from Jesus
He's the best friend you'll ever know
Many times I've turned to Him
So I know it to be so

When I am depressed
Rocking in my home
I turn to Him and say dear Lord
Please help me, I can't handle this alone

And I find this gentle Jesus
Is always there
He's the truest loving friend
He forever seems to care

Oh! What comfort it is
Him just to know
That when heartaches overtake you
To this Holy Man you can go

If you are sad and lonely
Try praying to Him
No matter what you've done
He'll gladly take you in

All the tears and heartaches
That I've been through
I never could have made it
Without this friend so true

Don't turn your back
On this gentle man
He'll always comfort you
When no one else can

He Reached Down

A man who believes in miracles
Prayed a prayer of faith one day
And Jesus Christ reached down and healed me
And took my pain away

This man Jesus performed miracles
Way back in Bible days
Will answer prayer and heal you
That's what the Bible says

Put your trust in Him
Expect your miracle to come
And as you are expecting it
Believe it will be done

Do not doubt that it can happen
Only believe it's true
Then when someone prays for you
It may happen to you

Many days and nights I suffered
With gallstones and pain
Now eight years has passed
The pain has never returned again

Oh! My brother and sister
Please believe it's true
For Jesus Christ has healing power
And some day may heal you

He Took Me In

I followed Satan
I was lost one day
Jesus picked me up
When I went astray

I took the wrong road
The road that led to sin
He washed me with His blood
And took me in

Now I am His
From sin I am free
All because He suffered
On the cross for me

Can't you love Him
For what He did for you
Read the Bible every day
For each word is true

He is with His father
He must weep because of sin
Turn to Him my friend
He'll gladly take you in

He Walks Beside Me

There lived a man long ago
That walked in the Holy land each day
He taught the people how to love
And also how to pray

He was so kind and gentle if you
Were a beggar made no difference to Him
Or if you were righteous
Or full of sin

He forgave every one
That was willing to repent
This Holy man to the earth
From God was sent

He asked the people to follow Him
And spread His gospel around
Oh! What a precious Savior
That walked on Holy ground

I'm so glad that one day
God led me to Him
He has forgiven me
And washed me clean of sin

Oh! Precious Lord Jesus
I couldn't make it without you
I bless the day
I found this friend so true

Walk beside me forever
As you promised to do
And I'll raise my hands forever
In praise to you

His Home In Heaven

He left His home in Heaven
He came to earth one day
He walked among the people
He taught them how to pray

He said to Mary Magdalene
Condemn you I won't do
Go and sin no more my child
Is all I ask of you

He walked among the poor
And the sick He healed
And while praying on the mountain
I'm sure He must have kneeled

Oh! Jesus how I long to see
You walk the earth today
If you could walk among us
I'm sure more often we would pray

Dear Jesus are you back of a cloud
Looking down below
Is the rain your teardrops
Are you weeping so

As I write my poems
Please let me try
To tell those who read them
Why you had to die

I Believe

I believe that the man Jesus
That died on a cross one day

Shed His holy precious blood
To take all sin away

I believe if we follow Him
And live as He wants us to

That someday when he comes back
He'll give us life anew

I believe if we try to help others
Those that are sick and in pain

I believe He will say
Well done when He comes back again

I believe He wants us to pray
For our enemies as well as our friends

Then He will reward us some day
When this wicked worlds ends

I Can't Make It Alone

When I awake in the morning
There's loneliness in my home
I need you Precious Jesus
I can't make it all alone

I wait for the phone to ring
Or a knock on my door
For it's not like
It used to be before

I go about my housework
And my cooking each day
But emotion overtakes me
And the tears won't go away

I walk out in the yard
I see a squirrel climb a tree
When God created him
He made him beautiful and free

Somehow I'll get through the day
Then will come another night
And as the days and years pass
God will make everything right

I Don't Walk Alone

When the sun is rising in the East
Lift your hands up high
And receive the precious love
That He has for you and I

Though I can't see Him
I know He's in my home
He'll walk beside me forever
And I'll never be alone

Make believe you can see Him
Walking by your side today
Remember He is always there
He taught us how to pray

Never mind what the world
Has to offer you
You are richer than a millionaire
For He walks along with you

Just think some folks
Don't have food to eat
And their only home is
On a concrete street

Oh! Thank Him for what you have
Thank Him for your home
Praise and thank Him each day
And you'll never walk alone

It Was Free

I'm not a millionaire
I'm poor as can be
But my Savior died
On the cross for me

There wasn't any cost
I didn't pay a cent
For my salvation
To the cross He went

No person on this earth
Ever loved me so
Without the Savior's love
I couldn't go on I know

Old friends and loved ones
Have all let me down
When I think I can't go on
I remember my Jesus I found

So take my hand dear Jesus
Catch my tears as they fall
For precious Lord and Savior
You're the truest friend of all

Let Me Kneel At The Altar

Let me kneel at the altar once more
Let me humble myself before you
Please Jesus let me understand
At the cross the suffering you went through

Let me pray for the sick and hungry
And for those who don't know you
Let me pray they'll hear the name Jesus
Before their lives are through

Let me forgive those who have hurt me
Let me pray for them too
For I know you would forgive them
If they asked you to

Before I arise from the altar
One more thing I must say
If I have hurt anyone dear Jesus
Please forgive me today

Precious Jesus I praise you
Thank you for dying for sin
Even though I am not worthy
Please Jesus take me in

My Lord, My God

Oh! Lamb of God what would I do
If I couldn't kneel and pray to you
Lamb of God how could I get through the day
If I couldn't kneel and pray

When my heart is breaking and the tears fall
You are the dearest friend of all
I turn to you and I humbly pray
Jesus please forgive my sins today

I feel your Holy presence around me all the time
Jesus use my hands I give them back to you
As I take your last supper of the bread and wine
I witness to others you're a Savior so true

I tell them how you healed me
And you heal others again and again
I tell them if they accept you
You will wash them clean of sin

Precious Lamb of God
You shed your blood on the cross
In agony you suffered
To save the lost

Many days my heart aches
And tears run down my face
Then I think of the tears you shed
The day you took my place

So thank you Precious Jesus
I know it had to be
And I can never repay
For the blood you shed for me

She Prays Alone

She sits beside the fireplace
Her hair is silver gray
She wonders why someone
Doesn't stop by to pray

She sits there all alone
Watching the flames rise high
With tears in her eyes she prays
To Jesus in the skies

He said I will never leave you
I'll always be there
So when you're sad and lonely
Just fold your hands in prayer

He's the only friend
That doesn't stay away
When you're old and lonely
And your hair is silver gray

She takes a handkerchief from her purse
And dries the tears from her eyes
Then bows her head to pray
To the Savior in the skies

Speak To My Heart

Speak to my heart dear Jesus
Tell me what you would have me do

Walk along beside me each day
Let me live as you'd have me do

Speak to my heart dear Jesus
Show me where I should go

To help some lonely person
Perhaps a stranger I do not know

Speak to my heart dear Jesus
Let me bring cheer each day

To some heartbroken person
That I may meet along the way

Speak to my heart dear Jesus
Let me tell others about you

Let me tell them they must repent
For that's what you'd want them to do

Take My Hand

Take my hand, walk with me
As I go along life's way
If you walk with me Dear Jesus
I will never go astray

Once I walked a crooked road
I was so far away from you
But I found the narrow road
Now I have a life that's new

Take my hand Dear Jesus
Don't ever let it go
For you are so kind and forgiving
The best friend any one could know

Walk with me forever
Walk with me each day
When I'm depressed and lonely
You will show me the way

I bless the day I found you
It turned my life around
I bless the day you came to me
Your name has such a Holy sound

Take my hand Dear Jesus
Walk along with me
If you stay by my side
From sin I'll always be free

I'll tell others about you, how you turned my life around
How one day you came to me and a new life I found

Take my hand Dear Jesus don't let me fall along the way
I couldn't live without you I need you every day

Temple Of Clay

While I live on earth
I live in a temple of clay
But I've given my heart to Jesus
So I'll live in a mansion some day

This earthly home of mine
Will someday crumble away
But I have joy in my heart
Though I live in a temple of clay

Someday I'll be with Jesus
And I'll leave this temple of clay
Jesus has promised this
And Satan can't take it away

So Satan you can't harm me
Though you give me pain
For I am looking forward
To seeing the Lord again

He'll keep me safe from harm
If I repent and pray
And my precious Lord
Will take me from this temple of clay

Try to find the Savior
Before you are old
Then when you leave this earth
You'll walk on a street of gold

You are living in a temple of clay
You'll always be alone
Take the Savior into your heart
And you'll never be alone

The Only King

As I sit in the twilight this evening
And I hear the whippoorwill sing
I think of a man who lived long ago
This one and only king

His kingdom is not of this world
He lives so far away
This man rules as king
In His home in Heaven today

Oh! I wish I had lived
In those days long ago
And could have known this Holy man
But it wasn't meant to be so

Now I read all about Him
In the Bible I have in my home
Where He says I'll be there
I will never leave you alone

So when others desert me
And they can't seem to forgive
I can talk to this man Jesus
Forever He still lives

Oh! The heartache and tears
That depresses me each day
Deserted by Christians
Why do they all stay away

So each day I try to go on
And fight depression and tears
For I know there is someone
That helps me get through my fears

This Sinless Lamb

This sinless man named Jesus
Will turn your life around
He's done that for me
The day this sinless lamb I found

He'll be there beside you
He'll remove sorrow from your heart
You won't have to be depressed and alone
From you he'll never part

Seek and you'll find Him
Tell others about Him too
Tell them He will do for them
What He has done for you

Don't let anyone tell you
That He doesn't live
My brother and sister he lived forever
And forever He forgives

But you must find Him now
Before the day you die
He's living up in Heaven
Somewhere in the sky

Open up your Bible
Read where they crucified Him
This holy sinless lamb
Died on the cross for sin

I couldn't live without my faith
That He still lives today
When depression overtakes me
I can always pray

Wipe The Tears Away

If you're sad and lonely
And the days go slowly by
Jesus understands
And He sees you when you cry

Jesus didn't promise
You're life would be a rosy hue
Do the best you can
Some day He'll reward you

Try to remember
Someone else is lonely too
Pick up the phone and call them
Then maybe someone will call you

Wipe the tears away
Start another day anew
Jesus died in agony
Because of His love for you

Do something nice
For some one that's alone
The Lord will see you
As He looks down from His Heavenly home

Two

The 1970s

This was Gramma's home she helped build in 1942 and lived in the rest of her remaining 62 years. This photograph was taken in the 1970s.

No Room At The Inn

"No Room At The Inn"

107.

They traveled on a mule to the city
And as they were going up - hill
"Mary softly whispered to Joseph"
I think I am going to be ill

They stopped at an inn in the city
the Inkeeper turned them away
So they stayed at a stable that night
And "Jesus" was born on the hay.

The Wise men came to adore him
the babe who was born that night
They presented him with gifts
While the Heavenly star shone bright

Soon he had grown to manhood
he Preached, he healed, he Prayed
And because he was Crusified
All Man kind can be saved.

Then One Sorrowfull day
he carried his Cross to the Hill
He died for you and I
It was his father's Will.

By: Helen O. Larson   Oct 1st, 1977,

October 1, 1977 – Age 66

The Birth Of Christ

G.

"The Birth of Christ"

They traveled on a mule to the city
And as they were going up hill
Mary softly whispered to her husband
I think I am going to be ill

He stopped at an inn in the city
the innkeeper said they couldn't stay
So they stayed at a stable that night
And "Jesus" was born on the hay

The wise men came to adore him
the babe that was born that night
The Wise - Men brought gifts to him
While the Heavenly star shone bright

Soon he had grown to Manhood
he Preached he healed he Prayed
And because he was Crucified
All Man - kind can be saved,

One Sorrowful day he
carried his Cross to the hill
He died for you and I
It was his Fathers Will

By: "Helen A. Larson"
1977

1977 – Age 66

37

The Vision In The Chapel

In the chapel one Easter Sunday
As I walked down the isle
I saw a vision of my Lord
With such a beautiful smile

And as I kneeled to pray
The vision became so clear to me
He said, though I live forever more
I died to set the sinners free

As I arose to go
I turned and looked at Him
He said again, I died to save the sinner
Please tell the world again

As I was walking out the chapel door
I heard Him softly say
Tell the people to turn to me
Then the vision faded away

So I give the message
As He gave it to me
He died to save the sinner
He died to set him free

1977 – Age 66

Three

The 1980s

Gramma is seen here with her husband, Ivar, in March 1987. He was to leave her on January 21, 1988 to start his journey to meet Jesus.

Stained Glass Window

"Stained Glass Window"

I dreamed I saw a Stained glass Window
  appear in the Sky.
It Split right through the middle
  and christ Stepped out on high

He was gazing down.
  I knew that he Saw me.
It Seemed he was Saying
  I died to Set you free.

His hands we at his Sides
  I saw his Nail Pierced hands
    when the Nails went through
  He didn't die for me alone
    he also died for you.

His face looked So Sad.
  Because People don't follow him
He was trying to Say.
  I'm coming back again.

So let's take this for a Warning
  and often Knell and Pray.
So We will be ready
  When he comes back Some=day

      By: Helen O. Larson.

Original Copy. March 1981 (·)

March 1981 – Age 70

Christ Lives

I know Christ lives
And I can talk to Him
Because He has promised
To forgive all sin

I wish I could make
Others understand
He suffered, bled and died
With a nail in each hand

It's so good to know
When skies are gray
That there's going to be
A better day

Now I feel so close
To Him today
Why don't you love Him too
For there's no other way

When I found Jesus
This I know
He washed my sins
As white as snow

Please take time out of your busy day
And talk to Him as you kneel and pray

If you have sorrows please turn to Him
Open your heart and He'll come in

On the cross He died to set us free
We must now believe what we cannot see

March 1985 – Age 74

I Am With You Always

Blessed Lord and Savior
For weeks at a time
You let me lay there sick
While you worked on my mind

Jesus you took away my sorrow
And said give them to me
For I died on the cross
So you could be free

Now at last I know
The agony and pain
That you suffered Jesus
That I might live again

Please keep me from judging
I've no right to do so
For you will judge one day
The Bible tells us so

I'll help support your Gospel
And feed your hungry too
For if you were here
I know that's what you'd do

I'll speak a kind word
I'll wipe a tear away
And I'll really try
To live the Bible way

Jesus, you have told us
To forgive we must do
For when you died for us
You forgave us too

I won't dwell on my sorrows
I'll forgive and pray
That you will touch my loved ones
And they'll turn to you someday

One day as I listened
It seemed I heard you say
My child I'll dry your tears
If you will kneel and pray

So with trembling legs
I kneeled beside my bed
Blessed Lord and Savior
You are arisen from the dead

My old life is gone
I am free from sin
Because of your love Jesus
I've been born again

May 7, 1985 – Age 74

My Friend

My friend lives in the sky
When I'm depressed or the same
He is always there
Jesus Christ is his name

He is my counselor
My guardian angel too
He is the best friend you can have
Do you have this friend too

When I have problems
Or troubles that pile high
I kneel and pray to my friend
Who lives in the sky

No matter what you've done
He will always say
Those who come to me
I will never cast away

So if you have troubles
And are also blue
Call upon this friend
He's always there for you

April 1986 – Age 75

44

When Jesus Lived

Lord Jesus, if I had lived when you lived
I would have traveled dusty roads with you each day
I would have listened as you told
Of your Father's house far away

I would have gazed in wonder as you laid your hands
On the sick and they were healed
I would have been so amazed at your power
At your feet I would have humbly kneeled

Lord Jesus, those people were blessed
They had you with them for a while
You were so compassionate and loving
You blessed every man, woman and child

Lord Jesus, if I had lived
In that country where you were born
I know on this earth
I would have never did any wrong

I have read in the Bible
How your Father sent you here
He must have loved us sinners so much
To send His Son so dear

Lord Jesus, stay close to me
I have taken you into my heart
Please walk with me forever
Never to depart

I know you're coming back
You promised to come again
So until that day
Please keep me free from sin

February 1987 – Age 76

The Good News

"The Good News"

Tell the World he has Arisen
    and he's alive to-day
He's Sitting On the throne with his father
    In his home in Heaven far away,

Since you know "the Good News"
    And you know it's True
Don't Keep it to Yourself
    Please tell others too.

Tell the World the cross is empty,
For he left it One day
Tell the World he will forgive them
    If they repent and Pray,

Tell the World "The Good News"
If they do good and Pray
He will take them With him,
    When he comes back that day,

    By: "Helen O. Larson" "Hope",
        March 1987,

March 1987 – Age 76

46

Mercy In His Heart

He left His home in Heaven
To come to earth one day
There's mercy in His heart
If we repent and pray

He grew up in the holy land
When as a babe He was born
Just the same as us He faced temptations
His heart with grief was torn

He went about doing good
He forgave all sinners too
And if you will ask Him
I'm sure He'll forgive you

Stop a moment and think
How He suffered pain
And because He died on the cross
Eternal life you can gain

Fall to your knees
Weep and pray
Ask the Savior to
Come into your heart today

June 1987 – Age 76

He Bled and Died For Sin

I dreamed I saw a vision
Of you hanging on the cross one day
And as you hung there bleeding
It seemed I heard you say

They took a hold of me
And nailed me to the cross
I gladly gave my life
For a world in sin was lost

Because I loved you so
I let them crucify me
Because you have followed me
From sin I have set you free

My father gave me life again
I'm living once more with Him
Stay on the straight and narrow road
And someday He'll take you in

You'll walk a street in Heaven
With sparkling gold it's paved
I'll come and take you there
If you accept me and you're saved

My blessed mother Mary kneeled
With tears streaming down her face
I know she would have gladly
On the cross taken my place

Follow me each day
Turn away from sin
And I'll take you with me
When I come back again

October 1987 – Age 76

I Found Jesus

I'm so sorry Jesus
I strayed so far away
I'm so happy Jesus
That I found you one day

My childhood wasn't happy
My parents didn't know God
So to get on the right road
For me it was so hard

So I took another road
The one that leads to sin
But through sickness and sorrow
I began my life again

I'll spread your word through my poems
I'm happy today
Because in a Pentecostal church
I found you one day

I know dear Jesus
The world is full of sin
But everything will be all right
When you come back again

December 1987 – Age 77

I Saw A Cloud Roll By

I saw a cloud roll by
As I sat on the terrace one day
And I wondered if Christ was behind it
As the wind softly blew it away

I thought if He could only come down
And stay a while and see
And end all the drugs, murders and crime
What a wonderful world it would be

And I kept imagining
That He was really here
It seemed I could
Feel His presence near

He would heal the sick
And those who could not see
He'd also heal the lame
And He would set the sinners free

But it was only in my mind
It didn't happen that way
So we will have to watch and wait
For that special day

January 1988 – Age 77

I Want Him

He has appeared to others
I want Him to appear to me
I want Him to take my heavy load
And carry it for me

I want Him to walk beside me
And to tell me of His love
I also want Him to tell me
Of His father's home above

I want Him to say dear loved one
I'll walk hand-in-hand with you
If you promise to live my way
You'll walk with me when life is through

Some day this great desire
Will be so real to me
I'll watch and wait always
For I'll walk the straight road for thee

As I end this poem
I feel His presence near
When all others forsake me
I'll have you Jesus dear

January 1988 – Age 77

I Wish You Were Here

I wish you lived on the Earth
I would walk along with you
You would heal me with your hands
Like you used to do

I would listen as you talked
As you told of your father's love
And I would also listen
As you told of your home above

I would walk the dusty roads
Just to be by your side
I would be so very happy
If with you I could abide

But I know it can't be so
I know it can never be
So I will watch and pray
Until you come back for me

Then my troubles all will end
You will wipe my tears away
So until that day arrives
I will live the Jesus way

January 1988 – Age 77

A Walk Through Heaven

I'd like to cross the silver lake
And see with my eyes

The land that Jesus
Told the thief was Paradise

I'd like to walk
That golden street

And feel the touch of gold
Beneath my feet

I'd like to see the gates
They say are pearly white

I'd like to see if stars
Come out at night

I'd like to see the mansion
That Jesus calls His home

So I could come back and tell it
To loved ones of my own

February 1988 – Age 77

Christ Still Lives

As I read my Bible
Christ comes alive to me
He dries the tears from my eyes
As I trust in thee

I read where He healed
The blind so they could see
I wish He was here now
I'd ask Him to heal me

Because of my faith in Him
I can take the heartache I know
He tells us to call on Him
And we will reap what we sow

So that's what I'm doing
I will forget the heartache and pain
I will spread His gospel
Until He comes back again

So Satan you can't hurt me
I'm telling you to stay away
For I have faith in God
So you can't touch me today

February 1988 – Age 77

Please Forgive

Lord my heart is filled with sorrow
Because I made you cry
Please forgive me Jesus
So I can live with you when I die

It seems I can see the cross
And your arms stretched out wide
Blood dripping from your fingers
As you gave up the ghost and died

I'll know you when I see you
By looking at your hands
Oh! Holy Son of God
You died in the Holy land

I look up at the clouds
And I imagine I see you
Oh! Blessed Lamb of God
Let me live one day with you

Let me tell others
About you're great love
How you're living with your father
On a throne above

February 13, 1988 – Age 77

Alive Forever More

"Alive Forever More"

An angel Walked through the garden
        rolled the Stone from the door
And "Jesus christ" Stepped Out
        Alive forever more.

He glanced at the lillies
        So Pure and white
Oh! if we could of Only
        Seen that beautiful Sight

The cross Or the tomb
        Couldn't hold that Savior then
His father gave him life Once More
        he lives, he lives again.

He ascended into the clouds
        But before he Went away.
He made a Solemn Promise
        that he'de come back Some-day.

Oh! believe in him my friend
        he'll turn your life around
I have had New Hope
        Since this "Jesus" I found.

He lives forever-More
        he watches over You
Read the Bible believe the Bible
        for every word is true.
        By! "Helen O, Larson"
        "Hope"   "age 78 yrs. Old,"

1988 – Age 77

56

Alive Forever More

An angel walked through the garden
Rolled the stone from the door
And Jesus Christ stepped out
Alive forever more

He glanced at the lilies
So pure and white
Oh! If we could have only
Seen that beautiful sight

He ascended into the clouds
But before he went away
He made a solemn promise
That He'd come back someday

Oh! Believe in Him my friend
He'll turn your life around
I have had new hope
Since this Jesus I found

He lives forever more
He watches over you
Read the Bible, believe the Bible
For every word is true

March 1988 – Age 77

Dogwood Tree

Every time I walk through the woods
And I see a dogwood tree
I think of the Savior who died
To set all sinners free

Every time I see a hill
I think of that dogwood cross
Where the Savior died
To save those who are lost

I picture Him walking and falling
From the weight of the cross that He bare
I wonder if they would have let me
Help Him if I had been there

At the top of the hill
They set the cross in place
They nailed His hands and feet
And agony showed on His face

Our Savior was tortured and beaten
With a sword He was pieced in the side
With a crown of thorns on His head
For the sinners he gladly died

How we sinners must hurt Him, do we make Him weep each day
He's always ready to forgive if we repent and pray

Our Savior died on the cross, we're not worthy I know
He shed His blood that day because He loved us so

So let's start our lives over and leave that road of sin
Let us walk each day the road that leads to Him

April 1988 – Age 77

Set My Heart Free

Set my heart free dear Jesus
Take away the fear and the pain

Replace it with love and joy
Let me be free once again

Set my heart free dear Jesus
Send someone to comfort me

All I want out of life dear Jesus
Is to be loved and be free

Set my heart free dear Jesus
This is always my prayer
Please send some of your love down

For I know you're living up there

Set my heart free dear Jesus
So it won't ache as it does today

This I humbly ask you
As I kneel and pray

May 1988 – Age 77

Because Christ Lives

Because Christ lives
I can face the pain

Because I know
He's coming back again

Because Christ lives
I can face the sorrow

Because I know there's going to be
A happier tomorrow

Because Christ lives
I can wipe the tears from my face

Because one day
On the cross He took my place

Because Christ lives
I can go on living

Because He's so
Loving and forgiving

May 24, 1988 – Age 77

Jesus Saves

Before I found Jesus
I was full of sin
Then one day someone
Told me all about Him

So if you have sins
Ask Him, He'll set you free
He'll forgive your sins
As He's forgiven me

He led me to a church
On a hill one day
Where the people know how to worship
And also how to pray

He died on the cross
For sinners you know
Oh! What a terrible death
What a painful way to go

He's living with his father
Somewhere in the sky
Repent and accept Him
Then you can live with Him when you die

November 1988 – Age 78

I Called On Jesus

I called on Jesus one day
When I was in pain and alone
And as I continued to pray
You were in my home

Dear Jesus you're always there
Whenever we need you
Jesus if we couldn't reach you
What on this earth would we do

Jesus you are wounded
In another way
When we turn to sin
And neglect to pray

Teach me how to love you
Teach me how to pray
Teach me to praise you
Each and every day

Make me ever thankful
I was born in a country free
Make me always conscious
That you died for me

Let me gaze up at the sky
You're in your Heavenly home
Please protect and comfort me
As I grow old alone

November 23, 1988 – Age 78

Let Me Walk With You

Let me hold your nail scarred hand
Let me walk with you some day
Grant me this prayer dear Jesus
When I pass away

Dry my tears precious Jesus
Heal my broken heart
Let me live with you some day
Never again to part

While I'm living on the earth
Send angels to watch over me
Give me courage to go on
Remind me I can pray to thee

Let me comfort someone ill
Let me call some lonely soul
Let me send a greeting card
To someone who is ill

Let me kneel and pray
Always thanking you
For being a faithful friend
That I can always turn to

Let me watch the clouds
As they roll by
They remind me always
You're in your home in the sky

April 24, 1989 – Age78

Untitled

When troubles cause me sorrow
And I don't know what to do
I know I can always
Kneel and pray to you

When my heart is breaking
And no one seems to care
I can always count on you
For you are always there

When sorrows weigh me down
And it seems I can't go on
I know I can depend on you
To keep me safe from harm

Why did you care so much
That you died for me
You were nailed on a cross
Made from a rough old tree

As I shed so many tears
Satan gets hold of me
He's angry because I worship you
Because you died to set me free

May 1989 – Age 78

Broken Heart

Broken hearts can be mended
I know they can in time
For the man named Jesus
Reached down and mended mine

Don't give up my friend
The pain will go away
For this man named Jesus
Will mend your heart someday

Just remember His mother
Had her heart broken too
When the Roman soldiers
Drove the nails through

She had to watch them
That crucifixion day
And it broke her heart
For they took her son's life away

Give your love to someone
Who is lonely and in pain
Then I know Jesus Christ
Will mend your heart again

May 1989 – Age 78

He Paid The Price

I dreamed I saw a cross
Up in the sky
And Jesus Christ was hanging there
For us, He had to die

A crown of thorns on His head
His face etched in pain
He let them take His life away
That we might live again

We do not own our bodies
Jesus bought them one day
And with His precious blood
Was the price He had to pay

This Lamb of God did for us
What no other friend would do
So my brother and sister
Let us love Him too

Be careful what you do
Be careful what you say
For He may be behind a cloud
And looking down some day

June 14, 1989 – Age 78

Lord I Have You

What would I do without you
How could I get through the day
Who could I turn to Jesus
If I couldn't kneel and pray

When my eyes fill with tears
And they run down my face
There's no one here on earth
That could ever take your place

What could I do dear Lord
When my heart is breaking in two
How would the tears go away
If I didn't have faith in you

When folks desert me
And I feel all alone
I sit and wonder why
They don't pick up the phone

Jesus you had a cross to bear
I know they crucified you
Please dear Lord help me
To bear my cross too

My faith in you helps me
To keep going each day
So thanks Lord I have you
When troubles come my way

July 12, 1989 – Age 78

Come Follow Me II

As I gaze at the beautiful sunshine
I know He's so close to me

And it seems I can hear Him say
Come follow me

He's always speaking to our hearts
If we will stop and hear

The master is saying to us
I died for you dear

Leave all your sinful ways
Come, walk along with me

Jesus I Have You

It's depressing to get lonely
Yes, I feel lonely each day
But then I think I am lucky
For I accepted Jesus one day

Now He's in my home
So lonesome I shouldn't be
For He is the truest friend
And He will never leave me

I can talk to Him
When no one else is here
For He's a faithful friend
And He's always near

What would I ever do
How could I go on
If He wasn't close
To keep me free from harm

So thank you dear Jesus
For being here each day
To comfort and protect me
As I go along life's way

August 8, 1989 – Age 78

Dear Lord Jesus

Dear Lord Jesus
Look down on me today
Send someone to comfort me
Please take the grief away

Dear Lord Jesus
I'm so all alone
Send a special friend to me
So I won't be alone

I go about my work
I make it through each day
I stop now and then
To wipe the tears away

I crochet, write and sew
And read once in a while
But I would like a friend
To make me smile

Dear Lord Jesus you bore your cross
So I'll try to bear mine
Maybe things will change
And someday I'll be fine

So until that day
I am asking you
To look down on me
And be the greatest friend I ever knew

December 1989 – Age 79

Four

The 1990s

Gramma is seen here celebrating Christ's birthday 1993. She is now 83, living alone, crocheting, and writing poetry to pass the time of day.

He Never Promised

He never promised a bed of roses
He said trials and tribulations would come our way
But He would help us overcome them
If we would always pray

This gentle man named Jesus
Let them drive the nails through each hand
What other person would have suffered
Such agony for his fellow man

He had to overcome temptation
Just like you and me
Resist the devil
And away from you He'll free

How wonderful it would be
If He walked the earth today
We would be careful how we lived
And take more time to pray

This same Jesus is coming back
With the Angels some day
Forever watch and wait for Him
For that's what the Bible has to say

June 23, 1990 – Age 79

Lamb of God

Blessed Lord and Savior
When tears roll down my face
I know you understand
For one day you suffered in my place

When some folks turn against me
And it seems they do not care
I kneel and pray to you
For I know you're always there

When I have heartaches
And I feel all alone
Precious Lamb of God
I know you're in your heavenly home

You said you would never leave us
And I know you do not lie
So it gives me courage to get through
The days that I cry

Lamb of God, Lamb of God what would I ever do
If I couldn't kneel and pray and tell my troubles to you

Thank you precious Jesus for suffering that day
And the debt you paid for me, I can never repay

I tell others about you, how you healed me one day
They don't seem interested and they slowly walk away

I long to be in your house and feel the power that comes from you
I love to sing you praises and raise my hands up too

Lamb of God, Lamb of God you died on a tree
But the cross is empty now for your father set you free

August 1990 – Age 79

Jesus Heals

"Jesus Heals"

When "Jesus" reaches down and touches you
   And takes away the Pain
Thank him my brother and sister
   Praise him he lives once again

Friends may not under-stand
   if you are sick they may not want to hear
Take courage my friend
   "Jesus" is always near

If the answer to your Prayers
   don't come right away
Just keep having faith
   And Pray again another day

If you are faithfull
   I truly believe.
The answer will come
   your healing you will recieve

One day you will Notice
   you're no longer in Pain
Then say Praise the "Lord"
   he lives once again

   By: "Helen A. Larson "Hope"

      Age 80. May 17th, 1991.)

May 17, 1991 – Age 80

He Walks With Me

He walks with me in the daytime
He's close to me at night
I couldn't go on without Him
In the darkness His presence makes it light

As I go along life's journey
It helps to know He's near
Oh! What a precious friend
In my heart I hold Him dear

This man's name is Jesus
He is everywhere
If you are sad and lonely
He is always there

Oh! Precious Lord and Savior
The day I turned away from sin
You didn't turn your back on me
You gladly took me in

Thank you Precious Jesus
For being a friend so true
When depression overtakes me
I always turn to you

June 7, 1991 – Age 80

Ye Are My Disciples

"Ye Are My Disciples"

Ye are my disciples
"Jesus" said one day
Go and spread my gospel
tell others about me each day

That's what each of us
has been commanded to do
Don't be hearers only for his Word is true,
Since I can't go and tell them
All about him
I'll send his message
through my Poems again and again

If you are able
to go and spread his Word
Please won't you do it
for the Name "Jesus" some have never heard

Just remember he commanded
and this we must do
Take time to tell others
for his gospel is true.

By: Helen A. Larson "Hope"
Age 80.
July 1st. 1991.

July 1, 1991 – Age 80

76

By The Nail Prints

"By The Nail Prints"

He didn't want to go to the cross
  he was much too young to die
But it was his fathers will
  So he died for you and I.

He let them drive the nails in
  and put the crown of thorns on his head.
The Roman soldiers thought that was the end.
  but he arose from the dead.

Oh! the agony he suffered
  his blood ran out of him
He made this sacrafize,
  to free us all from sin

His Blessed Mother Mary
  Kneeled beneath the cross and cried
Her heart was breaking
  for her beloved son had died

If I am ever fortunate
  and he appears to me
By the Nail Prints in his hands
I shall know him Instantly.

By: Helen A. Jarson "Hope" age 80
      July 12th, 1991.)

July 12, 1991 – Age 80

He Bought Me

My Savior bought me
With every drop of blood He shed
My Savior died
But He's no longer dead

My Savior bought me
In agony and pain
He died that day
That we might live again

My Savior bought me
A lamb that had no sin
My Savior bought me
That I might live again

My Savior bought me
The sky grew dark that day
It was His father's will
That He died that way

My Savior bought me
The crown of thorns pierced His head
My Savior lives
He's no longer dead

July 13, 1991 – Age 80

Resurrection Garden

I'd love to make a garden
So beautiful to see
I'd name it Resurrection Garden
And in the midst I'd plant a tree

I'd stand a cross at the entrance
Where all around it could be seen
And when folks walked by
It would seem like a dream

I'd plant some white lilies
On each and every side
As a reminder to all
That Jesus Christ once died

Oh! This Resurrection Garden
Would be famous everywhere
And folks would ask one another
Have you ever walked there

I'd dedicate this garden
A memorial to Him
This precious sinless lamb
Who died for sin

I know I can never make it
But this dream is in my heart
Maybe someone will read my poem
And the garden they will start

If they do, my greatest wish is
It will be where all can see
And that they will inscribe a plaque
In Jesus' memory

September 20, 1991 – Age 80

I Sent You

As I was praying I said
Your people are sick and hungry
Do something, please do
And God said, I did, I sent you

So if each of us
Don't do our part
How can we say that we
Love Jesus from our heart

There are sick and hungry
Right here where we live
If we don't do as He said
Will Jesus ever forgive

Jesus commanded us to
Take care of widows and fatherless too
How can we attend church and say
We are a Christian if this we do not do

They don't have to be a member
That's not what he said
To the hungry, sick, and lonely
We must be lead

If you know of someone sick and you don't do a thing
How can you kneel and pray to Christ the King

I try to help when I can but I am sick and lonely too
Remember, we must face our maker when this life is through

I can't go and tell them about Jesus but I can kneel and pray
And make photo copies of my poems and send them far away

1991 – Age 80

He Lives

The Savior came to earth
Such a short while to stay
Then they crucified Him
The sky was dark that day

They made Him carry his cross
It was heavy to bear
But He had to do this
For the soldiers were standing there

Then on Calvary Hill
On the cross He hung
He went to His death
His work on earth was done

While He was hanging
There was a thief on each side
And my Lord hung there
Until at last He died

They placed Him in a tomb
Rolled a stone against the door
The soldiers were sure
They would see Him no more

He walked out of the tomb
So holy and so fair
The lilies bowed their heads
When they saw Him standing there

My Lord was raised from the dead
He is alive once more
It happened just the way
That He foretold before

1991 – Age 80

During My Absence

During my absence I command you
To visit the sick and lonely too
He gave these commandments
To both me and you

In the scriptures it tells us
The people heard Him say
Do these things always
While I am away

If we know of someone sick
And we don't do a thing
How will we ever face
Christ the King

If we know of someone hungry
Give a dollar or two
But for the grace of God
That someone could be you

If someone needs a coat
Share your clothes with him
Jesus will say well done
When He comes back again

Visit the sick, feed the hungry
Can't you hear Him say
Remember I commanded you
Before I went away

February 3, 1992 – Age 81

He Walked The Earth

There was a man who walked the earth
Many, many years ago
He healed the sick and lame
The Bible tells us so

He walked on burning sand
He walked upon the sea
He left His home in Heaven
He did all this for you and me

Now we should believe
What the Bible has to say
He really lives, He really lives
In Heaven today

This holy man Jesus
Lived on earth one day
Now just for awhile
Then He'll come back someday

Yes, this holy man
Years ago He lived
And if you repent and pray
He will gladly forgive

Now He lives in Heaven
He rules by His father's side on a throne
Believe in Him, believe in Him
And you'll never feel alone

February 7, 1992 – Age 81

I Believe II

The Bible says one day
A vision you will see
And the Blessed Virgin Mary
Will appear to thee

It's in the scriptures
Read it someday
Then you'll believe in visions
That has appeared far away

I'm sure Sister Bernadette
Wasn't a mental case when she saw
The vision of the Virgin Mary
In that holy place

God can make a statue bleed
God can make a statue cry
God created everything
From His home in the sky

He said you will see a vision
Beloved do not fear
For in the last days a vision
Of the Virgin Mary will appear

Do not be a skeptic
Only believe it's true
Then maybe someday a vision
May appear to you

Get your Bible out
Read it from cover to cover
You will be surprised at
What you will discover

April 22, 1992 – Age 81

Christ The King

When the sun comes up in the east
And the robins start to sing
I think of a man who once lived here
His name was Christ the King

He went about doing good
Healing the sick along the way
He lives today, He lives today
He was born upon the hay

Though we cannot see Him
His presence is always near
He's a kind and gentle man
In my heart I hold Him dear

We raise our hands in praises
As the Hymns we sing
Forever praising this holy man
Jesus Christ the King

When my heart is filled with sorrows
And folks don't understand
I always turn to Him
This kind and gentle man

He lives my friend, He lives
And when the sorrows start
I give them all to Him
And He mends my broken heart

April 28, 1992 – Age 81

He Lives II

Many songs have been written
For so many years
About this man who someday
Will wipe away all tears

He must weep when His children
Turn away from Him
And go about their own way
Committing so much sin

Can't you hear Him calling
Please come back to me
Walk beside me always
I will set you free

Let me carry your burdens
Tell me what troubles you
I will wash you clean of sin
I will make you new

My heart is full of mercy
My heart is full of love
I'm living with my father
In Heaven above

April 1992 – Age 81

He Cares My Friend, He Cares

Try not to be depressed
Thinking no one cares for you
There's someone with a great love
He's gentle, kind, and true

Your miracle is coming
Just keep yourself in prayer
He'll answer one day
From His home up there

He cares my friend, He cares
And when sorrows get me down
I turn to the truest friend
I ever found

He cares my friend, He cares
Your miracle is on the way
Keep your faith in action
Continue to pray

He always answers prayers
He's gentle, kind, and true
Sometimes His answer is no
If it isn't good for you

He cares my friend, He cares
Don't give up and say
He doesn't care for me
For He cares each and everyday

May 1992 – Age 81

Let Him Catch Your Tears

You wouldn't want to give your son away
But I know of a man that did that one day
He sent Him to earth, a ransom for sin
And if we accept him He'll take us in

Oh! That kind and gentle man
Died one day but still lives
He sometimes heals the sick
All of our sins He forgives

Where could you ever find
A friend that's so true
For many friends on the earth
Desert and turn away from you

If you're sad and lonely
And the tears fall
He is holding His hand out
Let Him catch them all

Let Him catch your tears
He'll know what to do with them
Give all your sorrows
To this sinless man

May 1992 – Age 81

This Man Jesus

"This Man" "Jesus"   #3

There once lived a Man
    so Holy kind and true
Talk to this man in Prayer
    if you are sad and Blue

And do as he commanded
    be kind to every-one
Help to feed his hungry People
    some-day he'll say Well done

No Person wants to hear
    that you are sick and Blue
But he Will listen every-time
    he Won't turn away from you

This man's name is "Jesus"
    you can talk to him each day
He believes you when you tell him
    you are depressed as you Pray.

Each time I'm Blue I talk to him
    he listen's to what I have to say
When I tell him No one cares
    he Never turns away.

By: Helen O. Larson age 81.
    September 19th 1992.

September 19, 1992 – Age 81

89

He Walked On Burning Sand

"He Walked On Burning Sand"

This man Walked the Holy Land
    so kind and full of love
He told of his Father's home
    In "Heaven Above.

He Wore sandles on his feet
    As he Walked on burning sand.
Never On earth was there ever
    such a gentle Holy man.

He Preached the gospel truth
    he told the People then
If they Would Only believe he Would
take them With him when he comes
                    back again

Let's read about this sinless Man
    and the way he lived
He said to repent from sin
    for he's always ready to forgive.

He healed the sick each day
And the blind so they could see
And if We Pray and believe
    he May heal You and me.

By: Helen O. Larson — "See- age 82., Nov, 8th 1992.)

November 8, 1992 – Age 82

We'll Walk With Him In White

There will be no more sorrow
Through the day or night
When we hold His nail scared hand
And walk with Him in white

He will show us all the mansions
That are in His father's home
We will be forever with Him
Never to be alone

And on that blessed day
When our savior we meet
We will walk with Him in white
On that golden street

Never again will our eyes
Be filled with tears
Never again will we be
Full of fears

He will show us all around
It will be a glorious sight
When we hold His nail scared hand
And walk with Him in white

He told us to forever
Watch and pray
For we would see Him in the clouds
Coming back someday

He'll take us home with Him
He'll make all things right
Then we'll hold His nail scared hand
And walk with Him in white.

January 5, 1993 – Age 82

In Remembrance of Me

His disciples heard Him say
Do this in remembrance of me
Eat the bread and drink the wine
As you see it done by me

It must have been so sad
To hear the beloved Jesus say
That He would be crucified
And taken away

They didn't want Him to leave them
They loved this man who was a king
They knew if they parted from Him
Sadness it would bring

As they ate the Last Supper
They looked at one another that day
As if to say they didn't
Want their Messiah to be taken away

But the day they had dreaded
Soon came to be
And they remembered what He said
Do this in remembrance of me

It must have been so sad
To see Him in agony die
He was suffering that day
He died for you and me

July 3, 1993 – Age 82

He Left His Home In Heaven

"He Left His Home In Heaven"

He lived with "God" In "Heaven"
    before his earthly birth
He left his home in "Paradise"
    to live and walk on earth

He lived a poor and humble life
    he walked among the poor each day
He was always willing to heal
    those he met along the way

He spoke and made
    the lepers skin white as snow
And his healing power
    comes from "God" we know

Just think how fortunate we are
    that "God" sent him here to live
And how precious he is
    and so willing to forgive

This precious "Lamb" of "God"
    so "Holy" and "Divine"
And how greatfull I am, that
    I can call this "Savior" mine

By: Helen O. Larson
    age 83,,
        Jan 5th 1994,,

January 5, 1994 – Age 83

The Greatest Story Ever Told

The greatest story ever told is
About a baby boy born one day
There was no room at the inn
So He was born on the hay

God sent Him down from Heaven
To save a world from sin
He grew to be a kind and gentle man
Accept Him and He'll take you in

Oh! This gentle man named Jesus
Always went about doing good
And we must believe in Him
The Bible says we should

He traveled all the roads
In the Holy land
With only sandals on His feet
He walked on the burning sand

My brother and sister please accept Him
He'll wash your sins away
Only He can save you
There is no other way

He was a Prince in Heaven, His father had riches of gold
Yes, my brother and sister it's the greatest story ever told

On this earth He was poor just like you and me
He suffered and died on the cross to set all sinners free

This story will be told as long as this world exists
The greatest story ever told and they'll tell it just like this

January 13, 1994 – Age 83

The Prince of Peace

There was a man who lived one day
He was poor like you and me
He said if you want to be saved
You must believe in me

Oh! This man named Jesus
He preached, He healed, He prayed
And the miracles He performed
Left the people amazed

The miracles He performed
He still performs today
Just because He went back to Heaven
God never took His healing power away

He's living with His father
He sits on the thrown
Believe in Him my friend
And you'll never be alone

Oh! This lamb named Jesus
Came to earth from His Heavenly home
Tell your friends about Him
So they won't feel alone

When you feel no one cares and friends have deserted you
Just stop and talk to Him, this I often do

We do not know why troubles often come along
But to desert this Prince of Peace would be definitely wrong

When troubles overtake me and tears fill my eyes
I stop and fold my hands and pray to this Savior in the sky

January 15, 1994 – Age 83

Cross of Shame

They cut a tree down one day
And made a cross of shame
And a young man died on it
Jesus Christ was His name

They laid Him on the cross
And drove the nails in
God's only sinless son
Died that day for sin

And His mother Mary kneeled
Beneath the cross and cried
For on that fateful day
Her beloved son had died

They took Him down from the cross
And in a tomb He lay
But an Angel appeared
And rolled the stone away

God called Him back to life
And before He went away
He said to watch and wait
That He'd return someday

Yes, He hung on the cross
Blood flowed from His skin
He overcame sin and death
Now He lives once again

January 17, 1994 – Age 83

Just To Walk Where He Walked

I wish I could walk just once
In that Holy land across the sea
Where my Savior walked, preached and healed
And from demons set the captives free

Oh! Just to see the roads He traveled
Each and every day
Just to walk where He walked
As He traveled along to heal and pray

Just once to see the place
They call Manger Square
Just to know I walked where Jesus walked
When He lived there

Just to see Calvary Hill
Where they stood that rugged cross
Just to see where precious Jesus
Suffered and died for the lost

Just to kneel and sob
And break down and cry
For darkness covered the earth
As the Lamb of God hung there to die

January 25, 1994 – Age 83

I Have A Dream

I have a dream
There's a place I long to go
To the hill where Jesus died
Such a long time ago

I would climb that hill
Where they stood the cross
I would imagine I could see Him
As He died for the lost

I'd kneel at the place where they stood the cross
Sobbing and weeping for Him
Where through His hand and feet
They drove the nails in

I would picture the blood and water
My heart breaking in two
For we were so unworthy
But He died for me and you

I would try to vision
Where the thorns pierced His skin
And how on that cross
Our Lord died for sin

I would rise from the place
Where I had kneeled to pray
I would be sobbing and weeping
As I walked down the hill that day

Then I'd visit the tomb where they laid Him
I'd open the door and look in
I'd see an empty tomb
For He lives once again

Once again I'd return
To this land I love
And I'd tell them have faith
For He lives up above

Lord Jesus someday
This dream I may fulfill
And go to that land
And climb Calvary Hill

But I know my dream
Can never come true
It's only a dream on paper
So I leave my dream to you

January 28, 1994 – Age 83

The Crucifixion

In that land far away
And the place called Calvary Hill
When the Crucifixion took place
As the world stood still

And the clouds darkened
And covered the sky
All nature seemed to know
An innocent man was to die

God sent Him here to suffer
And give His life for sin
My friend, please accept Him
And He'll take you in

They sold His garments
For such a small price you know
It's true my friend, it's true
The Bible tells us so

One of His disciples turned traitor
And gave Him a deceitful kiss
But the prophet foretold
It would happen like this

Oh! This sinless lamb Jesus
Was willing to die
He said it is finished and gave up the ghost
As darkness covered the sky

February 19, 1994 – Age 83

Gentle Jesus

Oh! That gentle man named Jesus
Came to earth one day
To preach and heal and save
And take our sins away

God must have loved us very much
To send His only son
Now we must love and accept Him
For there is no other way

Oh! This precious lamb named Jesus
Suffered in our place one day
He gladly died upon the cross
To take our sins away

We must love and praise Him
Each and every day
He's worthy of our praises
For what He did that day

Oh! Jesus, precious Jesus
You died for a sinner like me
You let them nail you to the cross
You died so I could be free

You are the only savior
So let me lift my hands up high
Let me tell why you were crucified
Let me tell why you had to die

February 21, 1994 – Age 83

King of The Universe

"King of The Universe"

"God" sent him here to live
he had an earthly birth
And now to day Our Savior"
is "King" of the universe

"God" Has given him glory
he sit's by his right side
This humble child of "God"
who once was crucified

He died for sin One day
but "God" gave him life again
This "Lamb of "God",
who had no sin

He lives my friend he lives
And he's coming back some day
The "Savior" Promised this,
before he Went away.

So always watch and Wait
We don't know when it'll be
But when he comes and takes you home
from All sorrow you'll be free.

By: Helen O. Larson age 83,)

Feb, 27th, 1994,)

February 27, 1994 – Age 83

In That Land Across The Sea

One night so long ago
In a land far away
A baby boy was born
In a manger on the hay

The Shepherds came to see Him
Bringing gifts that night
They were guided by the star
And it's Heavenly light

He was born a Holy child
Sent from God above
To Mary and Joseph
To care for and to love

This darling little boy
Was born for one thing
To die on the cross and then
Resurrected to become King

Today He lives in Heaven
He sits on a throne
He's King of the Heavens
For Heaven is His home

He's coming back again
We will see Him someday
And then our loving savior
Will wipe all sorrow and tears away

So lift your hands up high
And sing praises to Him
So you'll be ready
When He comes back again

March 2, 1994 – Age 83

There's Room In Heaven

"There's Room In Heaven"

There's room in Heaven for one,
more angel to Walk that golden street
So let us live as "Jesus" said
then some-day those angels we'll meet

While we Walk on earth below
let's stay away from sin
Then when Our days have ended
"God" Will take us in

There's always room in "Heaven"
for One more angel so fair
So let us live for the day
when "God" will take us there

We Will see our loved ones
We Will hug and embrace
When we cross to the other side
and enter that "Holy" Place

So We'll keep on Praying
We'll help the sick and Poor
Then when we leave this earth
We'll enter "Heaven's" door.

By: "Helen A. Larson"

age 83, March 22nd 1994,

March 22, 1994 – Age 83

A Day To Remember

"A Day To Remember"

It's a day we must always remember
   It must stay in our memory
The day "Christ" suffered and died
   to set all sinners free.

We must never forget the pain
   And agony he was willing to stand
And the blood he so freely shed
   As they drove the spikes in each hand,

Oh! Jesus how much you loved us
   to do your Father's will
That crucifixion day you died
   On top of Calvary hill

Let it be forever embedded
   in our memory to stay
For if you hadn't died
   there would be no reason to pray,

Yes, it's a day to remember
   I'll tell others you died for them and for me
And that if they take you into their
                                    heart
   from sin you will set them free,

By: Helen O. Larson, May 20th 1994,

May 20, 1994 – Age 83

He's Knocking

"He's Knocking" #2

There lived a man so long ago
   who lived among the Poor
He wants to be your friend
   he's knocking on your door

Don't let him stand there and knock
   Please ask him to come in
He'll make you white as snow
   when he washes you clean of sin

Oh! This gentle man Named "Jesus"
   his heart is filled with love
He left his home in "Heaven"
   his father lives Above

Don't let him stand there and knock
   he's a friend so good and true
He wants to come in today
   to talk and Pray with you

So and open the door
   and tell him to come in
You will be so happy
   when you talk and Pray with him

By: Helen O. Larson · June 9th, 1994,)

Age 83.

June 9, 1994 – Age 83

106

He Died For You and Me

"He Died For You and Me"

A. M.

He shed his blood one day
   he did this for you and me
And if we repent and ask him
   from sin he'll set us free

Now can't you love him
   for what he did for you
If you accept him into your heart
   you'll be with him when life is
                through

There is no other Person
   Willing to go to the "Cross"
And give up his life
   to save those that are lost

Dear "Jesus" I am sorry
   you had to die One day
And also because it was
   such a Painfull way

I can't go and tell others
   About your Precious love
I can Pray they Will accept you
   for You live up above.

By: "Helen O. Larson" age 83,)
June 23 rd, 1994,)

June 23, 1994 – Age 83

Ocean of Mercy

"Ocean of Mercy"

"Jesus" said sinners would find
  an Ocean of Mercy in his heart
If they would follow him
  and from sin they would depart

Why don't you choose to follow
  this gentle "Holy" Man
That one day in "Galilee"
  he walked on burning sand,

He went about doing good
  he healed the lame and blind
I'm so at peace now
  since I met this "Savior" divine

He'll walk life's road with you
  he'll stick closer than a friend
He'll be with you always
  until your life will end,

No other Person on the earth
  cares about your sorrow dear
Let him lead you by the hand
  He'll drive away all fear.

                    By: Helen O. Larson,
                        age 83,

1994 – Age 83

He Came To The Earth

"He Came To The Earth"

He came to the earth
  a "Holy" Child One day
And the Animals stared in Wonder
  at the Baby "Jesus" On the hay.

He grew to be a child so Wise
  they found him in the temple one day
And the elders Were Amazed
  at the things they heard him say.

He grew to be a man
  a "Shepard" he became
Many books have been written about him
  "Jesus" "Christ" is his Name;

He was a "Preacher" a "Carpenter"
  and a fisherman too
Follow all his teachings
  And some-day he'll come for you

He is ready to forgive
  mistakes you made long ago
If you repent and are sorry
  And you tell him so.

By: "Helen O. Larson" March 23rd 1995,)

Age 84,)

March 23, 1995 – Age 84

Cross of Shame II

They laid the cross on the ground
And nailed my Savior there that day
That innocent Lamb of God
To take His life away

Then they stood the cross in the ground
Then Jesus hung up high
As His mother Mary watched
She began to cry

Her precious son named Jesus
Who had no blame
Hung there bleeding and in agony
On that cross of shame

He knew it was His father's will
That He should die that way
Now we must forever love Him
For what He did that day

Oh! Jesus, precious Jesus
It makes my heart ache
To think you gladly died
To save sinners from a terrible fate

Someday when we see Him
We will know that sacred man
We will be sure, for we will see
A nail print in each hand

April 9, 1995 – Age 84

Born To Die

Many books have been written
Many stories have been told about Him
How He was born to die one day
To save a world from sin

Open your Bible and read
Where He was born one day
And the animals stared in amazement
As the baby Jesus lay on the hay

When He was a holy child of twelve
They found Him in the temple one day
And the elders were astonished
At the things they heard Him say

He told them of His Kingdom
And the mansions in His father's house above
As He continued talking
He told them of His father's love

As the years passed He became a man
He fished, He preached, He prayed
One day He calmed the sea
When the fishermen were afraid

He often went off by himself to weep, to fast, to pray
It was always on His mind that He was born to die one day

Oh! That sinless lamb so Holy and so pure
And on that crucifixion day the pain He had to endure

So turn away from sin, take Him into your heart
Then someday you'll live with Him, never again to part

April 10, 1995 – Age 84

Creation Day

"Creation Day"

As another day begins
   I turn once more to you
I ask you to help me make it
   all day through

I look out the window
   and see the squirrels at play
Then I think of long ago
   of that creation day

The day your father in "Heaven"
   Willed the animals to be
Then they appeared alive
   he created wild — and so free

He created the birds and gave them
   wings so they could fly
Now when winter approches
   they take to the sky.

oh! The Power in his hands
   he created every-thing
"Jesus you are his only son
   and one day he crowned you king.

            By: "Helen O. Larson"
                  age 84, — April 11th — 1995.

April 11, 1995 – Age 84

He Walked The Roads of Galilee

Once there was a man that lived
In a land across the sea
And each day He walked
The dusty roads of Galilee

Oh! The compassion that He showed
As He laid hands on the sick each day
He healed many sick and afflicted
And He taught them how to pray

If only I could have lived then
And walked along with Him
That gentle man named Jesus
Who died for sin

Oh! How fortunate the people were
To live when He was there
That Holy man named Jesus
So gentle and so fair

I wish I had been among
The multitude at that time
And saw Him and heard Him preach
That Savior divine

But since I wasn't there
I can read about Him each day
And I can always talk to Him
For He's just a prayer away

April 13, 1995 – Age 84

Jesus Touched The Blind Man

"Jesus" "Touched The Blind Man"

A Man was sitting beside a gate
    he knew "Jesus" was Passing by
The "Bible" says he Called Out to him
    With a loud cry

Master I can not see
    Please lay your healing hands on me
"Jesus" Walked Over to where he sat
    he touched him and from blindness
                  set him free,
The man was no longer blind
    he sat by the gate no more
He didn't need to sit there and beg
    as he had done so many days before,

Oh! That Precious man Named "Jesus"
    healed folks along the way,
And that same "Jesus" lives and
    heals the sick and blind today

So have faith my friend
    he lives again he's Just away
Turn to him believe in him
    for he still heals today

        By: "Helen O. Larson" age 84,

        april — 21st — 1995,

April 21, 1995 – Age 84

114

He Paid The Ransom

"He Paid The Ransom"

Can't you hear the "Savior" say
I died to save a World from sin
Come to me — Please come to me
In my heart I'll take you in

Come out of the World my "child"
It has nothing to offer you
I will give you eternal life
if to me you'll be true

I hung upon the cross
in agony and Pain
Beloved I Paid the ransom
that you might live again

Today I ask you to accept me
repent from all your sins
Be true to me — Be true to me,
then a new life begins

I have Compassion in My heart
I'll love and comfort you each day
If you repent sincerely
and forever — Pray!

By: Helen O. Larson

Age 84 — May 1995,

May 1995 – Age 84

Come To Me With A Broken Heart

Can't you hear the Savior say
Though we're far apart
Don't bring me gold or silver
Come to Me with a broken heart

I will mend it for you
I will wash your tears away
I will comfort and protect you
For I died for you one day

All I ask dear child
Is for you to repent from sin
When you accept Me into your heart
Your new life will begin

Don't lay pearls or diamonds
At my feet one day
But always be faithful
And forever pray

Turn away from the old life
Take up a new life with Me
Then someday my child
My face you'll see

Come to Me with a broken heart
I will heal and comfort you
Turn to Me, love for Me
And you'll have a life that's new

May 13, 1995 – Age 84

The Prince of Peace II

Someday the prince of peace
Will be seen in the sky
The clouds will split in two
And He'll be seen by everyone

No matter when He comes
Be it day or night
He'll be wearing a robe
Of sparkling white

He will come then to
Take the faithful home
So live each day for Him
So you won't be left alone

No one will be able to learn
The song they'll sing that day
I believe angels will come with Him
To lead the way

He will take them to
His father's house above
They'll forever be with Him
Surrounded by His love

So take the time each day
To worship and pray
So you'll be among the faithful
He'll carry away

June 13, 1995 – Age 84

He Knows All

He sees every tear I shed
He knows every prayer I said

I turn to Him each day
As I bow my head and pray

He knows all the pain I feel
Some day He'll reach down and heal

From loved ones I had to part
Some day He'll heal my broken heart

I can carry on for each time
He listens to these prayers of mine

So when depression over takes me
I always turn to thee

Lord Jesus what would I do
If I couldn't turn to you

Since I know you're in your home
I don't feel so all alone

July 9, 1995 – Age 84

Resurrection Morning

Oh! That resurrection morning
When my Lord lived again
His Father raised Him from the dead
To save a world from sin

They laid Him in a tomb
But He did not stay
And that is why we now
Have an Easter Day

He walked out of the tomb
The lilies' bowed their heads
The sinless Lamb of God
Was no longer dead

If we tell Him we are sorry
And repent from all sin
He promises to forgive and love us
And He will take us in

We know the Bible says
There's mercy in His heart
He's always there to answer prayer
But we must do our part

Oh! That resurrection morning
Of so long, long ago
Will change the lives of them that believe
The Bible tells us so

1996 – Age 85

No Greater Love

One day they stood a cross
Upon a hill so high
They nailed the Savior there
For our sins He had to die

He was so pure and innocent
He was God's only son
He had to endure this suffering
Though no wrong He had done

How the nails made Him suffer
And caused Him so much pain
He bore the pain of the cross
That we might live again

He still bears the scars
In His sides and in each hand
And why He loved us so much
I try to understand

Soon they took Him down
And in a tomb He lay
But He was resurrected back to life
And He still lives today

So when you are sad and don't know what to do
Just talk to Him in prayer for He watches over you

We must always remember, He did what no other friend would do
The day He suffered and died, He proved His love for me and you

So ask this blessed Savior to come into your heart today
And never again be so busy that you can't take time to pray

April 10, 1996 – Age 85

The Resurrected Christ

Once my heart was full of sorrow
And I didn't know what to do
Then one day a friend of mine
Introduced me to you

Now when the tears fall
And I begin to cry
I always turn to
My friend in the sky

How could I ever make it
Through each lonely day
If someone hadn't told me
All I had to do was pray

Thank you precious Jesus
For forgiving all my sins
I'll always bless the day
You took me in

I know you are in Heaven
I know I can pray
Because you were resurrected
You will hear my prayer each day

Now when I look at pictures of my loved ones
And see their empty chair
One more day, one more time
I go to you in prayer

June 2, 1996 – Age 85

No Greater Love II

I have a faithful friend
He lives in the sky
And He's always close beside me
The days I cry

He proved His love
When He died that day
He has forgiven me
And taken my sins away

No greater love, no greater love
Then the love He has for me
And if He hadn't died
From sin I would never be free

Oh! How God must have loved us
To let His only son die that way
Now anytime I am lonely
I can always pray

No greater love, no greater love
Can ever be found
And this Lamb of God
Once walked on holy ground

So my brother and sister
Turn away from sin
Repent and tell Him you're sorry
And He will take you in

He will love and accept you
No greater love can be found
Then the love that comes from
A man who walked on holy ground

June 16, 1996 – Age 85

Cross of Shame III

Only one Christ
Who died for me
He hung on that cross
Made from a tree

Oh! How the thorns
Must have pierced His skin
He suffered that day
To free us all from sin

They pierced His sides
Tears rolled down His face
So we wouldn't suffer
He took our place

They drove the nails
Through His hands and feet
What a joy it will be
When my Savior I meet

Each time I see a cross
It always reminds me
That one day a sinless lamb
Died on a rough old tree

I feel sad when I know
He had no blame
And how He died
On that cross of shame

1997 – Age 86

Jesus, I Can Make It Through The Day

One moonlit night I gazed
Up at the sky
I knew you were in Heaven
And count the tears when I cry

You know when I am lonely
You know when I am blue
You also know each day
I pray and talk to you

Jesus if you were not there
What would I do
If in my troubled life
I couldn't talk to you

I know you are sitting
On a thrown in Heaven above
And if others desert me
I know I'll have your love

Thank you precious Jesus
For always being there
To comfort and console me
When I go to you in prayer

And as long as you
Listen when I pray
It makes no difference what happens
I can make it through the day

1997 – Age 86

Tears In The Chapel

I entered the chapel
And as I kneeled down to pray
Tears rolled down my cheeks
On this Easter day

I looked up at the cross
Where my Jesus hung
Then I began to cry
For this terrible thing they had done

They drove the nails through His hands
And through His feet too
The Savior died for me
He also died for you

He was pierced through His sides
His precious blood was flowing free
Then I cried again
For He had died for me

They laid stripes upon His back
And as I wondered why
I was overcome with sorrow
And again I started to cry

As I was about to leave
I cried once again
I shed tears in the chapel
For He gave His life for sin

1977 – Age 66

Your Home In Heaven

I wish I could part the clouds
And see the mansion you call home
When you were here on the earth
You often went to pray and be alone

When you were here on the earth
You mingled with the poor
And you always told them
You had lived before

You told them your father
Sent you here one day
You told the people to repent
And to forever pray

Oh! If only the nail prints
On your hands I could see
Oh! If only I could sense the pain
You bore to set me free

All I can do is try to imagine
The pain and suffering you took that day
Because you loved me you paid the ransom
To take my sins away

Precious Jesus, precious Jesus
Help me to understand
How you bore the pain of the cross
In the holy land

1997 – Age 86

Agony of the Cross

One day so long ago
On a hill so high
An innocent man was taken there
To hang on a cross and die

The sky grew dark that day
The sun didn't give her light
And those who loved that man
Knew what they were doing wasn't right

That sinless Lamb of God
How did they ever dare
To nail Him to a cross
As the people were watching there

Oh! That sorrowful thing they did
They had no shame
To crucify the Lamb of God
Who was without sin or blame

And as He suffered that day
They laughed and jeered at Him
As they saw the agony He suffered
From the nails they drove in

Oh! That precious Savior
Lives, I know He lives
Pray each day, pray to Him
He loves and forgives

Each time I see a cross
I think of that cross of long ago
When the Lord Jesus died
For God had willed it so

1997 – Age 86

Mercy In His Heart II

He left His home in Heaven
To come to earth one day
And He will take you there with Him
If His commandments you obey

There is no other person
That can do what He can do
His heart is full of mercy
He loves and cares for you

Oh! This precious man Jesus
He's the best you'll find
He will love and comfort you
Always keep this in mind

He heals the sick
The heartbroken too
Isn't it wonderful to know
One day He may heal you

Once again I say
If tears fill your eyes
Fold your hands and pray
To the Savior in the skies

When we pray to Him
He is always there
Every hour of the day
To hear our every prayer

1997 – Age 86

The Last Supper

Jesus called His disciples together
In the upper room
He told them He was going
To leave them soon

Jesus said one will betray me
As He said this they wondered why
He said because of this betrayal
On a cross I will die

And as He said that
A sad look appeared on His face
He said I reveal to you
This will take place

The disciples were concerned
They were going to be parted from Him
They knew this Jesus that they loved
Was going to suffer and die for sin

As He broke the bread and drank the wine
He said I must pay a ransom to set the people free
He said to them, do this always
In Remembrance of Me

Once a month in churches around the world
This sacrament is celebrated to honor Him
This holy sinless man that
Died on a cross for sin

1997 – Age 86

I Will Be With You Always

I will be with you always
Wherever you may be
If you are depressed and lonely
Just kneel and pray to me

This is what the master said
And I know He does not lie
He sees every tear and heartache
From His home in the sky

He will be there forever
He'll always be very near
So build up your faith my friend
For He is a friend so dear

No other person on this Earth
Can ever take His place
His heart is full of mercy
He has a kind and gentle face

My friend put your trust in Him
He will never let you down
When others leave and forsake you
He can always be found

I will be with you always
He meant every word He said
He's living again my friend
One day He rose from the dead

September 22, 1997 - Age 86

I Am With You Always II

I am with you always
Can't you hear the Savior say
If you keep my commandments
And you always pray

Take me in to your heart
Walk each day with me
And if you sin and repent
I'll forgive you and set you free

It is in the Bible
So I know it's true
And Jesus will do
What He said He'll do

He's alive in Heaven
He's no longer dead
Yes my friend He'll do
Everything He said

I am with you always
Can't you hear Him say
I'll be close beside you
Every night and day

And the day's you cry
Once again He'll say
Give all your burdens to me
And I'll wipe your tears away

I am with you always
My child, have no fear
I am with you in sorrow
For I am always near

September 22, 1997 – Age 86

The Cross and Calvary Hill

"The Cross And Calvary Hill" 6 "Verses"
"sent in"

Don't make a "cross" of "Silver"
don't make One of "Gold"
For once there was a "Wooden Cross"
and a story to be told.

They grabed a young Man
and Nailed him to the "Cross" one day
They thought it Would be the last of' "Him"
but his Father gave him life again

If you want to Wear a "Cross"
around your "Neck" One day
Make it a Wooden "Cross" for on it
they took a young Man's life away

Oh! That "Cross" that "stood"
On "Calvary Hill" so long ago
It's true I know it's true
the "Bible" tells us so.

He lives yes Jesus lives in "Heaven"
he "sit's" on a "Throun"
And we repent and "Worship Him"
some day he'll take us to his "Home"

This "Man "Jesus" who died
because he loved us so,
And he suffred deeper "Pain"
than We Will ever know.

(sent to the Twins)

By: Helen O. Larson October 16th 1997,)
Age 86,)

October 16, 1997 – Age 86

Come Follow Me III

When He walked the earth
The people heard Him say
Come follow Me, come follow Me
As He went along the way

It was many, many years ago
He lived and preached each day
His heart was full of love
And He taught the people how to pray

He was a carpenter
He was a shepherd too
Follow this man's teachings
For someday He may heal you

He's the same Messiah of long ago
He lives in Heaven today
He's always there to listen
To us as we pray

Oh! This precious man named Jesus
Will forgive us if we sin
So we must live close to Him
Then someday He'll take us in

Listen and you will hear Him say
Come follow Me, come follow Me
Live my way and always pray
And from sin I'll set you free

December 14, 1997 – Age 87

The Master Is Calling

The Master is saying come to me
I'll forgive you and wash you white as snow
I'm always here my child
To hear your prayers you know

If friends have forsaken you
And you are lonely tonight
Pray to me, please pray to me
And I will make everything right

I'm living in a mansion
My home in Heaven above
Call on me in troubled times
I'll freely give my love

Can't you hear the Master saying
One day I went to the cross
I let them crucify me
To save sinners who were lost

Listen and I know you'll hear Him say
I am the same Messiah that walked the earth long ago
I do not change, I never change
The Bible tells you so

Yes, the Master is calling
If we will listen to Him
He will take us home
When He comes back again

1997 – Age 87

A Lamb Was Slain

If you can walk up Calvary Hill
Kneel down and pray
And try to imagine the pain He suffered
On that crucifixion day

Let the tears fall
From your eyes
Today this sinless lamb
Lives in a mansion in the skies

Oh! That blameless man
That had no sin
Suffered the pain caused
By the nails they drove in

And as you're kneeling there
Ask God to pardon you
For the sins you've committed
All your life through

He will understand
And forgive you I know
Then say another prayer
Just before you go

Walk back down the hill
Tell others where you've been
Tell them you climbed Calvary Hill
Where a young man died for sin

January 29, 1998 – Age 87

Hill of Shame

When the Sun goes down
And stars twinkle in the sky
My thoughts turn to a land far away
Where a young man was condemned to die

Oh! My heart aches when I think
Of that hill so far away
Where Jesus gave His life
To take our sins away

On that day He suffered
Agony and pain
He did all this so
We could live again

Oh! Precious Lamb of God
He had no blame
But on that crucifixion day
He died on a cross on that hill of shame

My heart aches when I think
Of that hill so far away
And as He suffered and died
The sky turned gray

I wish I could go there
And see where He died for me
His father willed it to be so
It was destined to be

1998 – Age 87

I'll Spread Your Gospel

As long as I can write
And as long as I can see
I'll help spread your Holy Gospel
With my poems, for you set me free

I feel so honored
That you have chosen me
To write about your son Jesus
And also that I can pray to thee

They say my poems offend them
That's what some people say
But it makes no difference to me
So I'll write about you again today

Precious Jesus you healed me once
And you healed me again one day
So I'm a witness of your healing power
And I thank you as I pray

I tell about my healings
To people I sometimes meet
I tell it to those in buildings
And I tell it to those on the street

Just give me the words
And I promise you
I'll go on writing them
For your gospel is true

1998 – Age 87

Jesus of Nazareth

Jesus if I had been at the cross
Tears would have rolled down my face
To see your nail pierced hands and feet
You died for the human race

You were so holy and pure
Without sin or shame
But you gladly died
Though you were without blame

Jesus I know you died
For all sinners like me
You suffered and died at the cross
Made from a rough old tree

Your blessed mother must have knelt down
Her heart breaking in two
Because of the terrible thing
They were doing to you

Dear Jesus, stay close by my side, walk along with me each day
Let me feel your presence as I fold my hands and pray

Dear Jesus I want you to know, with you I am never alone
I'll go on living for you, then someday you'll take me home

Jesus if I had been at the cross
I would have knelt with your mother too
I would have been praying and weeping
Because they were crucifying you

Please forgive me Jesus for straying so far away
But since I believed in you, I'm trying to live your way

1998 – Age 87

Our Lord Jesus Christ

He walked on the burning sand
Healing the sick and lame
To save the sinners souls
That is why He came

A lady touched His garment
She was healed that day
And she humbly thanked Him
As she slowly walked away

He told His apostles
He was leaving them soon
As He ate His last supper
In the upper room

He said one would betray Him
Each said Master is it I
And one did betray Him
For He had to die

One day He was with the crowd
And a blind man cried out to Him
Master please heal my eyes
So I can see again

His blessed mother Mary
Was at the cross that day
She was heartbroken as they took
Her beloved son's life away

1998 – Age 87

He Lives, He Saves, He Heals

Oh! That precious man named Jesus
Had lived so long ago
It's true, I know it's true
The Bible tells us so

He went about healing the sick
And the blind so they could see
And I know someday He'll reach down
And once again heal me

Oh! That precious man named Jesus
Is living up above
He's so kind and gentle
His heart is filled with love

He lives my friend, He lives
In a mansion He calls home
Talk to Him, pray to Him
And you'll never feel alone

He's the same Jesus
That lived so long ago
He healed me one day
And that is why I know

Forget what the world has to offer
Jesus offers something you can't buy
So take Him into your heart
And you will live with Him when you die

1998 – Age 87

When The Savior Returns

When the sky splits in two and
The Savior comes back someday
There will be no more tears
He has promised to wipe them away

There will be no more wars or killings
No more abortions or rape
For the power the Savior has
Is all that it takes

No more floods or earthquakes
No more drugs will there be
He's promised to end all of these
When He comes back for you and me

No more alcoholic drinks
No more suffering with pain
He will end all these forever
When He comes back again

No more heart attacks or cancer
No more suffering with pain
He will end all these forever
When He comes back again

No more hunger in the world
No more watching a starving child die
No more tears or sorrow
When He appears in the sky

1998 – Age 87

The Master Is Calling II

Listen and you may hear
The Master calling out your name
If you have sinned He will forgive you
And He'll love you just the same

Can't you hear Him softly whisper
Repent and turn back to me
I suffered and died at Calvary
To set you free

Makes no difference what you've done
Please come back to me
My child I'm calling out your name
And from sin I'll set you free

Please accept me into your heart
And leave your sinful way
All it takes is to say you are sorry
And to forever pray

You will be so happy
If you walk in my ways
I will send my love down to you
If you give me prayer and praise

The Master is calling out your name
Listen and you will hear
Just as you are, come to me
And I'll accept you dear

1998 – Age 87

The Gentle Shepherd

Long ago in a country
Far across the sea
A young shepherd named Jesus
Died for you and me

He tended His sheep
Each and every day
Then one lamb was missing
It left the flock and strayed away

The Bible tells us that
He was a kind and gentle man
He left the flock and went
To find the missing lamb

The Bible clearly states
He went about doing good
He knew one day He was to die
On a cross made of wood

He healed the sick and blind
He forgave them their sins
This gentle shepherd named Jesus
Will return once again

He taught the people to be kind
And to always help the poor
Then one day they would live with Him
Yes, live forever more

1998 – Age 87

Born To Die II

He left His home in Heaven
God sent him down from the sky
Can't we leave our sinful ways
For this man who was born to die

He was just a young man
He wanted to live like you and me
He didn't want to go to the cross
But His father willed it to be

He could have called ten thousand angels
To come and rescue Him
But He did His father's will
And was crucified for sin

We cannot see our Lord
But maybe He's looking down
And sees a sinful world
As He looks around

Can't we change our ways
And take more time to pray
Then we will be ready
When He comes back someday

Yes my friend
He was born to die
But He was resurrected back to life
And He's living on high

1998 – Age 87

For Them That Believe

If you want a healing
And I'm sure you do
It's for those that believe
That Jesus can heal you

As you go to Him in prayer
Just believe He hears you
And as you are praying there
Ask Him to forgive you too

He'll forgive all the sins
You've made throughout the years
As you are praying, thank Him
As your eyes fill with tears

His heart is full of love
You can start over again
And you will feel His love
As you are praying to Him

You will be so happy
You are free from sin
Oh! This blessed Jesus
Is coming back again

One day He reached down
From His home above
He touched me with His nail scared hands
His heart is full of love

April 19, 1998 – Age 87

Nail Prints In His Hands

Can't you hear the Savior say
There's nail prints in my hands
Read about it in the Bible
Then you will understand

Can't you hear Him say
They took hold of me one day
I was just a young man
But they took my life away

They made me carry
That heavy wooden cross
I suffered and died in agony
To save sinners who were lost

On that day my father
Turned His back on me
But I knew I was dying
To set all sinners free

Now I'm living in Heaven
My father gave me life once more
And I'm the same Jesus
As I was before

When I come again
You will understand
For I will show you
The nail prints in my hands

September 20, 1998 – Age 87

A Holy Child Was Born

"Walking the Trail of Tears"
"A Holy Child Was Born"
One Evening so long ago
a Holy Child was born upon the Hay,
And Now 2000 years later
We celebrate his Birthday.
His Proud Parents wrapped Him.
In clothes to Keep Him Warm.
Now We start celebrating his Birth
early Christmas Morn.
The animals gazed at Him
With wonder in their eyes
as the Heavenly Star shone.
and twinkled in the skies.
oh! That Holy Babe grew to a Man
grew up they may One day,
and that is why we
have a Savior today
Let the Church Bells ring
let Music be everywhere.
Proclaiming the Wonderful years
of the Birth of Jesus so fair.
Yes Christmas is a Holy Day.
forget all gifts and things.
For this Wonderfull day.
Is the Birthday of a King

Copyright 1998, Helen O. Lawor
All Rights Reserved
Written Nov, 6th 1998

November 6, 1998 – Age 88

The Light of The World

Soon it will be Christmas
The Birthday of the babe born on the hay
This precious babe grew to be a man
And He's the light of the world today

Let us assemble together
And sing praises to Him
For this holy man Jesus
Is coming back again

Don't worship Santa
And the Christmas tree
But sing, kneel and pray
For He died to set us free

When your heart aches
And friends turn away
Just talk to this man Jesus
He will listen as you pray

It's okay to send greeting cards
To those you love
As long as the message reminds them
They are to celebrate the Holy One alone

Yes, it's drawing very near
When church bells will ring
Calling the faithful to come
And worship Christ the King

November 8, 1998 – Age 88

If You Have Mercy

Jesus said if you have mercy
And help the sick and poor
Then I will have mercy
On you forever more

If you see an elderly person
As you go along life's way
Take a few minutes to show kindness
Each and every day

If you see a child
Crying on the street
Maybe he has had
Nothing to eat

Take a few minutes
To talk to him
Give him something to eat
Then he won't cry again

If you see an elderly man
Sitting alone on a bench one day
Please sit down beside him
As you go along life's way

Remember what Jesus said
Have mercy all your life through
And then when you need comfort
I'll be merciful to you

November 13, 1998 – Age 88

I Believe III

I believe what is in the Bible
That you lived on the earth one day
I believe Lord Jesus, I believe
You hear me when I pray

I believe you healed the sick
And the blind so they could see
I believe one night long ago
You reached down and healed me

I believe we should
Always worship you on high
I believe you are a friend
So faithful in the sky

I believe you ate your last supper
Before you went to the cross
I believe you came to the earth
To save those who in sin was lost

I believe you were placed in a tomb
And there you were supposed to stay
I believe your father gave you life again
And you were resurrected one day

I believe you're coming back
To take your faithful home
To forever live with you
And never again to be alone

November 25, 1998 – Age 88

The Angel Announced His Birth

The Angel appeared in the sky
To announce His birth
God had sent His only son
To be born on the earth

His father in Heaven
Has a Kingdom up there
So the Lord Jesus is the son
Of a King so fair

He was sent to the earth
And we must believe in Him
If we pray and keep His commandments
He will take us home with Him

He was just a babe
Lying in the manger that night
And the animals gazed at Him
Such a glorious Heavenly sight

The star in the sky
Gave a bright light
A Holy Baby born
On a cold December night

Let's keep Christmas for Jesus
Let's sing and worship Him
Then when He returns to the earth
We will be ready for Him

November 29, 1998 – Age 88

If You Need A Miracle

If you don't believe in miracles
And you say they are not true
My friend when you need one
They will become real to you

If like some other people
That say they ended one day
And there are no more miracles
Since Jesus went away

I know what I am writing
I believe in them
For one day I received a miracle
From Jesus Christ the man

Oh! My friend let your faith
Go up to Him each day
Ask Jesus to heal you
As you pray

Jesus Christ healed me
Eighteen years ago
Miracles still happen today
I know, I know, I know

You don't believe in miracles
You will believe if you need one
Pray to Jesus and believe
And you may be healed by God's Holy Son

December 4, 1998 – Age 88

Waiting For Jesus To Return

While we are waiting
For Jesus to return someday
Let us assemble together
To worship and pray

He will wipe away
All the tears that are shed
And replace them
With joy instead

There will be no more drugs
Murder or rapes
If we repent He will
Forgive all our mistakes

The Sun will seem more brighter
The sky more blue
When He returns
For me and you

The grass will seem
To be more greener then
When He returns
To the Earth again

So let us forever
Worship and pray
While we are waiting for Jesus
To return some day

December 6, 1998 – Age 88

One More Time I Come To You

Dear Lord Jesus
I come to you in prayer
I know you are listening
For you're always there

As I come to you
Again and pray
I ask you precious Lord
Please help me today

I need help for my body
And help for my mind
I know you will answer my prayer
Because you are kind

I have come to you
Many times in the past
I know you will heal me
And the healing will last

Thank you precious Jesus
For listening one more time
And bringing healing
To this body of mine

Thank you precious Jesus
For taking me in
Thank you precious Jesus
For healing me again

December 10, 1998 – Age 88

They Crucified My Lord

They crucified my Lord
They buried Him one day
They put Him in a tomb
And there they thought He'd stay

But an angel came along
And rolled a stone from the door
And my precious Lord walked out
Alive forever more

He went about healing the sick
And the blind so they could see
He didn't stay in the tomb
His father set Him free

He called His disciples
To the upper room
He told them that He
Would be leaving them soon

He said He would return
So they must watch for Him
When this gospel of the kingdom is preached in all the world
He would return again

Yes, He lives, my Savior lives
And He saves and heals today
He's waiting for you to call on Him
So why don't you take the time to pray

December 10, 1998 – Age 88

His Tender Touch

He healed me one day
I was suffering so much
He reached down one day
With His tender touch

I'll forever thank Him
Each and every day
For touching me so gently
And taking the pain away

It's wonderful to know
That we can call on Him
And when we need a healing
We can pray to Him again

All the pain is gone
That used to grip me
For one day Jesus reached down
And healed me

So many days I suffered
Racking pain grabbing me each day
Then someone prayed for me
And Jesus took the pain away

I'll tell others about my healing
In my poems that I write
How someone prayed for me
On that unforgettable night

December 11, 1998 – Age 88

He Holds My Tomorrow In His Hands

Put your faith in the one
Who holds tomorrow in His hands
No matter what lies ahead
Have faith in this man

His name is Jesus Christ
And His promises are true
Pray, worship and believe in Him
Remember the promises He has made to you

Never mind what the world says
Forget what they say
Repent from all your sins
For he's coming back someday

Yes, He holds tomorrow
In His hands today
Isn't it wonderful to know
We can contact Him when we pray

Live for Him, please live for Him
Repent of all evil things
There's going to be a better tomorrow
When He returns, King of Kings

So always be faithful
Be kind to everyone
Then one day you will
Live with God's Holy son

January 14, 1999 – Age 88

I Write In His Name

I write about this man Jesus
That had no blame
But they grabbed hold of Him
And crucified Him just the same

They laid the cross
On the ground one day
They drove the nails through
Then stood the cross up that day

As they watched Him die in agony
With His blood dripping to the ground
I've heard the dogs licked it up
As the people stood around

What a sad day it must have been
What a cruel thing to do
But He gladly bore the pain
He paid the ransom for me and you

It must have been so sad
To see Him hanging there
The people must have been weeping
But the Roman Soldiers didn't care

Oh! Precious Lord Jesus
When I see a cross
It reminds me of the one
You died on for the lost

January 22, 1999 – Age 88

The Christ I Serve

He's the Christ I serve
Let me introduce Him to you
He will turn your life around
Life will become anew

He's just above the clouds
Maybe He's looking down
Perhaps He doesn't like
What He sees as He looks around

Turn your life over
You can start again
He will love and care for you
If you turn to Him

Accept this Christ I serve
There is no other way
Don't wait until tomorrow
Do this today

The Christ I serve
Is gentle, kind and true
You'll be glad you accepted Him
It's the only thing to do

This Christ I serve
Is coming back someday
Accept Him into your heart
Forever worship and pray

January 23, 1999 – Age 88

Christ Is The Answer

If your heart is breaking
And you don't know what to do
Turn your life over to Christ
He will see you through

Forget about the world
And all material things
Pray each and every day
To the King of Kings

He's the answer to your problems
He'll never turn you away
Let me say it once again
Pray, please pray

I found Him when I was lonely
I found Him when I was blue
He'll keep you in His tender care
Each day He'll see you through

Material things don't interest me
As they did a while ago
Only Christ who died for sin
As the Bible tells us so

Oh! My brother and sister
Please take my advice
Seek the Christ I worship
Let Him take over your life

January 23, 1999 – Age88

If You Need A Miracle II

Maybe you don't believe in miracles
You will if you need one someday
When the doctor can do no more
You'll ask someone to pray

And you will ask the great physician
To please look down on you
You'll pray with tears in your eyes
To this one so kind and true

Jesus Christ is the name
Of the one that can heal you
You will plead with Him
And ask Him a miracle to do

Yes, someday my friend
When others can do no more
You will turn to the one
Who lives forever more

Oh! My friend please listen
To what I have to say
For this same Jesus reached down
And touched me one day

He took all the pain
That was grabbing me
Yes, the Lord Jesus
From pain set me free

January 27, 1999 – Age 88

A Hungry Baby Cries

Does Jesus weep each time
He hears a baby cry each day
Crying out from hunger pains
His little body wasting away

His mother looks on with tears in her eyes
She has no food for him day after day
Must God's children suffer
While the rich throw money away

When they come before God
Will He forgive them one day
For not sending food
To the hungry far away

I send donations
I help when I can
Please won't you do the same
For these people in a far away land

Remember Jesus said one day
Take care of the little ones
If we stop and listen we'll hear
The same words from God's holy son

Yes the children are hungry
Surely we can spare a dollar or two
I'm going to send a donation
I'm asking the same of you

February 28, 1999 – Age 88

Only Jesus Can Forgive

Call upon the only one
That can forgive your sins
Ask Him to forgive you
Start your life over again

He died one day
So from sin you could be free
He offers you His love
And it's free

He went to the cross one day
But He arose again
Pray and ask Him to forgive you
And He will take you in

The Bible says He's kind and gentle
He may be looking down on you
You will be so happy
The rest of your life through

This precious Lord
Is coming back someday
He'll appear in the clouds
To take His own away

You will feel free from worry
You will be happy to pray
Accept Him into your heart
Do this today

March 2, 1999 – Age 88

His Rainbow

One day as I looked up
I saw a rainbow in the sky

And overcome by emotion
I began to cry

And beneath the rainbow
It seemed I saw Jesus' face

It seemed He was crying
Because of the human race

The colors were so pretty
It seemed I asked Jesus why He cried

It seemed He said the world is wicked
And for them I gladly died

Jesus, please forgive us
I'll pray they'll seek you too

And when we leave this earth
We'll forever live with you

March 7, 1999 – Age 88

My Savior Lives

My Savior lives today the Bible tells us so
He arose from the tomb
He lives, He saves, He heals
I know, I know, I know

When we are sad and lonely
We can contact Him
He's always there to hear our prayer
Again and again

Oh! How fortunate
We have this Savior divine
He always hears your prayers
And He always hears mine

Because He died
From sin I can be free
And so I thank Him for
What He did for me

I must tell others
I must teach each day
How He suffered and died
To take our sins away

April 6 & 7, 1999 – Age 88

My Savior Lives II

A lamb was slain one day
On that old wooden cross
Where they took Jesus' life away
He died for the lost

Many people must have kneeled
At the foot of the cross that day
As He hung there and suffered
As His life slipped away

Many tears must have been shed
On that crucifixion day
He died but lives again
Yes, He's living today

Can't you love Him
For what He did for you
This Holy son of God
So kind and so true

He's now with His father
He arose from the tomb
He reigns up in Heaven
In the Kingdom Room

Let us forever worship
And pray
To the Lamb of God
Who arose one day

April 10, 1999 – Age 88

The Crucified Christ

The Apostles loved this man Jesus
Of so long ago
They didn't want Him to leave them
But His father willed it so

They knew He was going
To die on the cross one day
And that His body would be taken down
And carried away

They wished that
Would never happen
But it had to be so
To set all sinners free

Then came the time
For Him to die
They knew His mother Mary
Would break down and cry

Then came the day
They nailed Him to the cross
An innocent young man
Dying for the lost

April 16, 1999 – Age 88

The Dogwood Cross

They say the cross was made
From a dogwood tree
Where Jesus suffered and died
For you and me

I saw a dogwood tree in my back yard one day
The leaves were shaped like a cross
Just to think Jesus died there
To save those who were lost

If I could walk in my back yard again
I'd take another look
At the tree that they made a cross
Out of, to crucify Him

Each blossom had four petals
And a red spot in each of them
It looked like a drop of blood
Like the blood that dropped from Him

And in the center there was
A round golden ring
To represent the crown of thorns
They hung on our King

The dogwood tree blooms in April
And Easter comes in April too
So I believe the legend
Of the dogwood tree is true

April 17, 1999 – Age 88

A Place Called Heaven

There is a place called Heaven
It must be beautiful there
Where everyone is so happy
And the Angels are so fair

Where the streets
Are paved with gold
And it is often said
That people never grow old

Where Jesus lives
And reigns each day
And He hears our prayers
When we pray

He sits beside His father
On a thrown
And someday He will come
To claim His own

He hears all our prayers
In the Bible it says so
So we must keep on praying
He answers some I know

So let us each day
Pray and worship Him
Then He will take us to His home
When He comes back again

April 19, 1999 – Age 88

In The Garden

Jesus sat in the garden
He knew He was going to die
I think He sat there praying
To His father in the sky

I know He must have thought
About the apostles that time
He knew that soon He would leave them
Just for a time

I know Jesus must have been thinking
I have to leave this earth
For He was born here
It was a Holy birth

Jesus was so good
And He was so kind
But He had this terrible death
Always on His mind

I love the song in the garden
It's about Jesus too
I love all the songs about Him
I love to sing them through and through

Each time I hear that song
It touches my heart
The same as that other hymn
How Great Thou Art

May 13, 1999 – Age 88

He Walked The Earth II

He walked on the earth
Many, many years ago
It's true, I know it's true
The Bible tells us so

He was a kind and gentle man
Performing miracles each day
And the Bible says
He taught the people how to pray

If He lived on the earth
We could walk with Him each day
We could watch as He healed the people
And took their sickness away

Oh! That blessed Jesus
His heart is full of love
But we can contact him
For He's in His home above

If all the people in the world
Would follow Him each day
And stop and pray to Him
Then peace would come again

Oh! Lord Jesus, Lord Jesus
You're so precious I know
And if you lived here today
All the wickedness would go

June 1, 1999 – Age 88

The Light of Christ

Let the light of Christ shine on you
As through the day you go
It will always light your way
All the day through

If it seems to be dark
And the sun don't shine
Let His light always guide you
He will show you the way every time

Many people turn to Him
When it's dark and they can't see
Let His precious light shine for you
I let it shine for me

Darkness often comes
And we can't find the way
Again I say to you
Let His light shine on you each day

If we didn't have His light
We would be lost each day
So let the light of Christ
Shine on you each day

If your days are filled with darkness
And you think you can't get through
Keep yourself in prayer
Let His light shine on you

June 1 & 2, 1999 – Age 88

This Gospel of The Kingdom

This gospel of the Kingdom
Must be preached everywhere
Each person must hear it
We must help them through prayer

Some have never heard
What Jesus had to say
In those distant lands
So far away

He said it must be published
And go into the world each day
He said tell my people
They must always pray

He said wherever this gospel is preached
Signs and wonders would take place
He said into all the world
To every race

Always remember everyone
Must have a chance to hear
Preach this gospel to everyone
To those far and near

Again I say this gospel of the Kingdom
Must be preached everywhere
It must first be preached
Before I can come

June 14, 1999 – Age 88

The Gentle Jesus

Once there lived a man named Jesus
So many, many years ago
He lived, I know He lived
The Bible tells us so

So long ago He lived
In the Holy land
With only sandals on His feet
He walked on burning sand

He was a shepherd
And tended His flock each day
And became very upset
When a lamb strayed away

He was a minister
And told about His father's home
Some days He went away for awhile
He wanted to be alone

Oh! This gentle man named Jesus
Was so loving and kind
And a man like Him
Isn't easy to find

Yes, this gentle Jesus
Will return someday
We must always
Watch and pray

June 17, 1999 – Age 88

The Blessed Mother

One day so long ago
In a country far away
There was a girl named Mary
She was a virgin the Bible has to say

God called her one day
To be the mother of His son
And her life as a virgin
Had just begun

One day God said to Joseph
Don't be afraid to take Mary for your wife
For that which she is carrying
Is a sacred life

She was to be hailed
By people everywhere
People would turn to her
Every day in prayer

Today she is known as the mother
Of the Lord to whom we pray
So let us always remember her
In our prayers each day

Yes, she is a saint
She lives in Heaven above
She is so holy and fair
And her heart is filled with love

June 22, 1999 – Age 88

Keep My Commandments

Love one another as I have loved you
The people heard Him say
Keep my commandments
Each and every day

I command you to give freely
As I have given you
Always love your neighbor
As I love you

Visit the sick and elderly
During my absence too
Do a kind deed for someone
And it will come back to you

If you see a child crying
Stop and help him too
For some day another child may be crying
And it may be a loved one of you

If someone needs a coat
Give him one of your own
Hug them and talk to them
And tell them they're not alone

Do all you can to help
Someone that's in need too
And always remember a loved one of yours
May someday be in need too

July 3, 1999 – Age 88

I Can't Live Without Him

I cannot live without Him
The days would be lonely and long
He's always close beside me
He forgives me when I'm wrong

When things don't go right
And I don't know what to do
I call on this man Jesus
And He sees me through

I love to write about Him
I also love to pray
Pastor Gooding told me
God chose me to do this one day

When all the people
Don't seem to care
I know I can always
Go to Him in Prayer

Oh! My precious Lord
When the sky is blue
I know I can always
Talk to you

So once again tonight
I will say a prayer
And I know you will hear me
I know you're always there

August 5, 1999 – Age 88

Show Me
The Nail Prints In Your Hands

If anyone tells me
He is Christ the man
I will say to Him
Show me the nail prints in your hands

Show me you can
Perform miracles too
Unless you can do these things
I won't believe you

The Bible says many will come
And claim to be He
Show me the scars on your sides
That were there when you died on that tree

Show me how you parted to waters
So the army could go through
Prove to me you can do these miracles
If you can, then I will believe you

Show me how you
Can change water into wine
If you can do all these things
Then I'll know you are the Savior Devine

If you can't perform these miracles
And all the things I asked you to do
Then I'll know you are not Christ
And what you said wasn't true

August 13, 1999 – Age 89

Judas Betrayed Jesus

One of the apostles
Betrayed Jesus one day
He told the Roman Soldiers
Listen to what I say

I will walk over
Keep your eyes on me
And the one that I kiss
It will be He

Then he walked over
And kissed Jesus the man
And then the soldiers knew
It was Jesus the man

They laid the cross
On the ground
While those who loved Jesus
Cried as they stood around

Now we all know
On the cross He died
On that terrible day
He was crucified

His name was Jesus
And for a few shackles of gold
He traded the life of Jesus
It has been told

August 13, 1999 – Age 88

He Is Risen

Oh! The pain He suffered
And the crown of thorns on His head
And they thought when He died
He would remain dead

But in a few days
God called Him from the tomb
He wasn't in there very long
He was resurrected very soon

He smiled at the lilies
So white and so pure
And now my Lord
Lives forever more

Some day He'll return
To the earth again
So we must always pray
And watch for Him

When He returns He will be
So holy and so pure
And He will be with us
Forever more

When He returns
He will wipe our tears away
So make sure to always
Pray, pray, pray

August 15, 1999 – Age 88

Come Follow Me III

When He was on the earth
He was gentle as could be
And the people heard Him say
Come follow me

This gentle man named Jesus
Was so kind and true
He went about doing good
Each day through

He walked among the poor
He healed the sick and blind
He laid His hands on the sick
Time after time

We must always follow Him
Each and every day
We can always contact Him
He isn't far away

Oh! This man Jesus
Lived here at one time
He's our only Savior
He's the Savior Devine

Yes, we must always
Follow Him each day
We must always
Take the time to pray

August 27, 1999 – Age 88

Cross On A Hill

Oh! That cross
That stood on a hill long ago
Brought heartache
To His mother I know

It stood there that day
For all the world to see
Where Jesus died
For you and me

He took all our sins
And diseases that day
So long ago
When they took His life away

Oh! The pain that He bore
How He suffered then
So that one day
We could live again

Precious Lord Jesus
We can never repay
What you did for us
On that terrible day

Let us forever
Worship and pray
And give thanks for
What you did that day

September 2, 1999 – Age 88

If Jesus Lived

If the Savior lived
In the Holy land today
Maybe I could board a plane
And fly to that country far away

I could see Him do the miracles
That the Bible tells us He did then
I could follow Him around
And see Him do them again

I could hear Him
Tell about His father above
I could see this man
That has so much love

I could see the place
Where they say He was born one night
I could hear the people tell
About the star that shone so bright

But I know I can't go
So far away
But I can forever and ever
In my home pray

I can see the healing
That He does today
And to the holy man
I can always pray

September 24, 1999 – Age 88

When Your Heart Is Breaking

When your heart is breaking
And you don't know what to do
Pray to the Lord Jesus
He will see you through

Turn to Him
Each and every day
You will find that soon
Your heartaches will go away

Sometimes sorrow comes
To each and everyone
It's so comforting to know
We can pray to God's Holy Son

I have found this to be so
He will bless and comfort you
And you will soon realize
That each day you can get through

Once in each life
Heartache comes sometimes
I know this to be true
For one day it came to mine

Once again may I tell you
This I must say
Turn to the Lord Jesus
He will see you through the day

September 29, 1999 – Age 88

That Blessed Savior

He lives in Heaven with the angels
His father lives there too
If you pray to Him
He will answer you

Oh! If only He could
Live on the earth today
If we could have been there
When He taught the people how to pray

He is so gentle and
His heart has mercy too
Just to see Him in person
And to walk along with Him too

But we can read about Him
And what the Bible has to say
When He lived on the earth
Way back in yesterday

They kept singing He lives, He lives
And I know He does too
He lives in my heart
How about you

Oh! My precious Savior
I'll keep writing about you
As long as you give me the words
For I know you are true

October 9, 1999 – Age 88

His Name Is Jesus

Once there was a man
That died on a wooden cross
He gave His life one day
To save sinners who were lost

He arose from the dead
He's living today
And some day we can live with Him
If we repent and pray

Often I think of that cross
Where He died for you and me
Yes, the Bible says He died
So from sin we could be free

I wish I could go
And see that hill of shame
Where a young man without sin
Died there just the same

I wish I could go
And walk on that Holy Land
And see all the places that
Were visited by this Holy man

I know I can never go there
But I can go to His house and pray
To this holy sinless man
That died there one day

October 14, 1999 – Age 88

He Lived Long Ago

Let me tell you about a man
That lived so long ago
He lived on the earth one day
The Bible tells us so

This man's heart is full of love
You can contact Him if you pray
He has left the earth
But He lives today

Let me tell you
How He taught the people to pray
When He lived on the earth
Way back in yesterday

Oh! The healings He performed
He healed the blind so they could see
I know He lives and heals today
For one night He healed me

Oh! This Holy man
He is Lord of all today
If you are sick my friend
Ask someone to pray

Ask Him to touch you
With His healing power
He can perform miracles
Any day or any hour

October 14, 1999 – Age 88

189

My Savior Lives III

He was born in a manger
He grew up one day
He began to heal people
Taking their sickness away

He also tended sheep
In the pasture each day
Then one lamb was missing
It had strayed away

He was a carpenter
And made wooden things then
He was a preacher
He taught people then

He taught the people
How to pray
And the people followed Him
Each and every day

He forgave them their sins
He told them to repent too
But one sad day
His earthly ministry was through

One day He died on a cross and
Although His earthly ministry was through
My Savior lives again
He has a life that's new

October 25, 1999 – Age 89

190

Until He Takes Me Home

I know He will watch over me
For He's sitting on a throne
I know He will protect me
Until He takes me home

I know He wants me
To praise Him each day
I know He also wants me
To forever pray

I know He wants me
To help the hungry far away
I know He wants me
To remember them when I pray

I know He wants me to tell
People He healed me one day
I know He wants me to go to
His house just off the highway

I know He wants me
To call some lonely soul
I know He wants me
To pray for someone old

I know He wants me to pray
For those that are alone
I know He wants me to do these things
Until He takes me Home

December 20, 1999 – Age 89

My Father's House

My Father's house is a place
Where people assemble to pray
Try to go to His house
Each and every Sunday

It's a place so Holy
Where people can sing
As they sing those old familiar hymns
Tears to my eyes they bring

It's a place where you can
Kneel at the altar and pray
And also listen to what
The preacher has to say

It's a place where you meet
And chat with loved ones there
My Father's house is
A place of prayer

Try to go to His house
As often as you can
To sing and pray to Jesus
This Holy man

My Father's house is so holy
You can feel it as you open the door
Be sure you go there
More often than before

December 30, 1999 – Age 89

Five

The 2000s

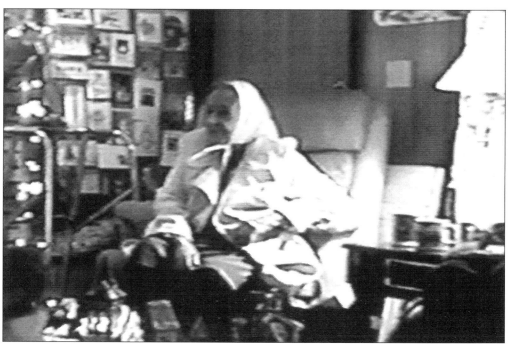

Gramma is pictured here at the author's home celebrating Christmas day 2000. On October 24th she had reached the milestone of 90 years.

He Overcame The Cross

He was crucified one day
They nailed Him to a cross
He hung there and suffered
As He died for the lost

They took His body down
And placed it in a tomb
But soon He left that
Dark and gloomy room

Yes my friend He died
To save the world from sin
And He is living now
Yes, He lives once again

He's the same Jesus
That walked on the earth long ago
I read it in the Bible
That is how I know

Now we must worship Him
And raise our hands up high
For this sinful world
He was willing to die

Yes my brother and sister
He died for the lost
But He lives once again
He overcame the cross

January 13, 2000 – Age 89

Jesus Will Help You

Jesus loves every one
No matter the color of his skin
He will love you and
Forgive you of all sin

Don't let anyone tell you
That He doesn't live today
For He lives forever more
And hears you when you pray

He is a very kind
And gentle man
Tell Him your heart aches
And He will understand

I turn to Him
When I am blue
Why don't you do the same
He will help you

Oh! This precious Jesus
Hears us as we pray
And if He wasn't there
I couldn't get through the day

Once again tonight
I'll go to Him in prayer
And thank the living God
That His son is always there

2000 – Age 89

He Prayed In The Garden

In a little town
Far across the sea
A young man named Jesus
Died for you and me

Oh! This precious Jesus
That was God's only son
He prayed this cup would pass
But He had to pay the ransom

He prayed in the garden
He didn't want to die
But they nailed Him to the cross
Beneath a dark sky

Soon it came the day
He would die for the lost
He suffered pain and agony
He died on the cross

He is living now
Yes He lives once again
He shed His Holy blood
He died to save us from sin

Always remember
He died that day
This sinless Jesus suffered
To take our sins away

April 24, 2000 – Age 89

The Little Wooden Cross

One day the mail came
There was a package for me
And when I opened it
A little wooden cross I did see

I will wear the little cross
Each and every day
I will cherish it forever
And never throw it away

It reminds me of another cross
Made from a large tree
When my Lord died on it
So from sin we could be free

Each time I look
At the little cross
It reminds me that
Jesus died for the lost

The little cross was made
By a man that lives far away
His name is Paul Barbour
And he sent it to me one day

So the little cross he sent me
Has come to me to stay
It was a beautiful gift
From someone far away

June 4, 2000 – Age 89

Does Jesus Cry On Christmas Eve

Does Jesus cry on Christmas Eve
Because some people forget Him
Some teach their children about Santa
And not about Him

Does He cry because
Of all the Christmas lights
And some people forget
About that first Christmas Night

Does He cry because
They think about the Christmas tree
And not about Him
Who died to set the sinners free

Does He cry when they eat
And forget to say a prayer
Don't they know He said
I will always be there

Does He cry
Once more again
Because they forget
He came to save the world from sin

Let us always remember
That first Christmas Night
When Mary laid Jesus in a manger
Wrapped in swaddling clothes of white

December 7, 2000 – Age 90

Jesus
I Will Make Your Name Known

I will write poems about you
I will make your name known
I will tell them through my poems
That you're in your Heavenly home

I will make sure the name Jesus
Appears in the poems I write
I'll continue writing if I
Have to stay up late at night

I want the name Jesus
To go all around
I want the people to know
Jesus is the truest friend I ever found

Yes, I'll make your name known
Each time I write each day
I want everyone to know you
So I'll send my poems far away

Yes, Jesus you are Holy
And you have a lot of power
I think of you every day
All day, every hour

Yes, Jesus I'll go on writing
I'll spread your Holy name
I'll tell the people if they accept you
They will never be the same

June 11, 2001 – Age 90

Couldn't Help Falling In Love

Elvis I love you
And soon we will meet
Together hand in hand
We will walk God's golden street

Meet me at Heaven's gate
And open it for me
Please Elvis be singing Amazing Grace
For it is my favorite Hymn you see

I have lived a long time
And loved you over half my years
When you sing How Great Thou Art
To my eyes it brings tears

Introduce me to Jesus
Such a good friend He's been to me
Always there when I needed Him
And now will set me free

Your fans still miss you
But not as much as I
And soon we will be
Together in the sky

I am now listening to your CD
Whatever that is
With my son Raymond
His visits with me I will miss

My time on God's Earth
Is getting short
I am so happy that
Your records and tapes I bought

They comforted me so
When my spirits were down
I would sit and listen
As they went round and round

My grandson Joel
Was born on January 8th
The day you were born in Tupelo
He and Tonya will soon have their fourth

My son Raymond and Ramona
Were married on the 16th of August
Such a sad day in history
The day you were called to leave us

I cannot drink
And I cannot eat
I can only lay here
Can't even feel my feet

Over the years almost seventeen hundred
Poems I have been writing
Some of you, some of Jesus
Others of my life, family and any happening

As I go to sleep
And this poem closes my book to you
I will be dreaming
Of meeting my love Ivar, my son Paul, Jesus and Elvis you too

Written May 16, 2005
Age 94 years, 6 months, 25 days
October 24, 1910 – May 18, 2005

Gramma Larson has left the building

Although Gramma wrote this poem to Elvis
it is the last poem she wrote that mentions Jesus
The author and his mom hope you have enjoyed her poems.

Ray's – Images of America series by Arcadia Publishing

The Lost Villages of Scituate: In 1915, the general assembly appointed the Providence Water Supply Board to condemn 14,800 acres of land in rural Scituate. The hardworking people of the five villages were devastated. By December 1916, notices were delivered to the villagers stating that the homes and land they had owned for generations........

The Scituate Reservoir: In 1772, portions of Providence received water through a system of hollowed out logs. By 1869 the public voted in favor of introducing water into the city from the Pawtuxet River in Cranston. By 1900, it was clear more, and purer water was needed. A public law was approved on April 21, 1915, creating the Providence...

West Warwick: By 1912, the citizens of the western portion of Warwick had been talking about secession. They possessed all the mills on the Pawtuxet River and were largely democratic, while the eastern section was primarily republican. Finally in 1913, the town of West Warwick was incorporated and became the youngest town in the ......

Foster: Originally incorporated as part of Scituate in 1731, became a separate community in 1781. The town was named in honor of Theodore Foster, a coauthor of the bill of incorporation. By 1820, the population topped out at 2,900 and then sharply declined. The population would not surpass the 1820 figures until 1975.

Pawtuxet Valley Villages: Between 1806 and 1821, a dozen mills were built on the Pawtuxet River, shaping the economy of surrounding villages. The mills provided a livelihood for the villagers who settled in the valley and drew immigrants looking for a better life from Canada, Italy, Portugal, Sweden, and other faraway countries.

Coventry: On August 21, 1741, the area west of what is now the town of West Warwick was incorporated into the Township of Coventry. The railroad would traverse Coventry in the mid-1800s, providing the gristmills, sawmills, and farmers with a quicker way to send their goods to market and to receive supplies in return.

Gramma Larson Remembers series
by Wolf Publishing

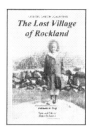

The Lost Village of Rockland is a book of photographs and documents with captions, featuring poems and tales by Helen O. Larson. She tells her story of growing up in the small New England Village of Rockland, in the Town of Scituate, Rhode Island in the early 1900s. She writes about having to suffer the agony of seeing her village......

Diary of Love Poems is the second book of the *Gramma Larson Remembers* series. It is a story of a love that began on a bus in 1956. It continued until her husband Ivar passed away 32 years later. However, Helen's love for Ivar did not end then. It carried on for another 17 years until she left to meet him on May 18, 2005.

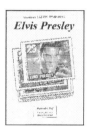

Elvis Presley is the third book in the *Gramma Larson Remembers* series. Her love for Elvis began in 1956 when she bought her son Raymond a portable record player with four 45 RPM records. One of the records was *Love Me Tender*. Through the years the boy born in a two room cottage in Tupelo, Mississippi rocked his way into her.....

Famous People, Family and Friends is the fourth book in the *Gramma Larson Remembers* series. She wrote her first poem in the summer of 1923 at the age of twelve. In her later years she picked up the handle of being called Gramma Larson. During her 82 years of writing rhymes, she wrote about many things. This book is broken down into three..

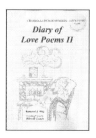

Diary of Love Poems II is the fifth book in the *Gramma Larson Remembers* series. It continues the love story that began on a bus in 1956. They were married in 1957 and their love sustained for another thirty-one years. Although Ivar died in 1988, her love for him did not die. It was unrelenting for another seventeen years.

More Titles by Wolf Publishing

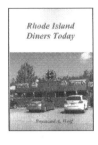

Rhode Island Diners Today spotlights 50 diners remaining in the state the author located after a great deal of research. He visited each one from Woonsocket to Wakefield and Burrillville to Block Island. The purpose of this book is simply to determine the location of all the diners in Rhode Island. There was no intention to rate the food or service.

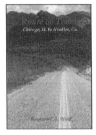

Route 66 Today: Chicago, Il. to Needles, Ca. is a book of 223 color images with captions. The journey begins with breakfast at the famous Lou Mitchell's Restaurant in downtown Chicago. It then heads west to pass the Gemini Giant in Wilmington, Elvis in Braidwood, and Abraham Lincoln in Springfield before cruising into Missouri.

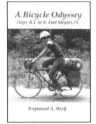

A Bicycle Odyssey: Hope, R.I. to N. Fort Meyers, Fl. began with a thought from my daughter Donnalisa as she spoke the words; "Wouldn't it be terrific if we all had ten speeds and we biked up to Uncle Paul's next year." You see my brother Paul, at the time, resided in Watertown, N.Y. Everyone thought we were crazy and would never do it.

World War II is an accounting of what John E. O'Hara went through during the war years. He joined the Civilian Conservation Corp in 1939. Then on December 7, 1941 the Japanese bombed Pearl Harbor. In the spring of '42 he boarded a bus. His destination was the Navy induction center in Providence, R.I.

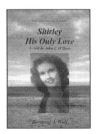

Shirley, His Only Love is a story about a lifetime love affair. It began as a passing glance on a sidewalk in Providence, R.I. in the late summer of 1948. John gives a history of growing up, joining the Navy, and being discharged. As a civilian he moved to New York City to follow his dream of being a photo engraver.

To order any of Ray's books visit: **www.raywolfbooks.com**

About the Author

Raymond A. Wolf, with his wife Ramona, and Zoey the cat, lives in the Village of Hope, in the Town of Scituate, Rhode Island. He is a graduate of Scituate High School and worked for AAA for 28 years. He then entered a new career as a manager of TJ Maxx and finally retired after 13 years. Now he just researches and writes books.

Ray belongs to six local historical societies and is a member of the board of directors of the Pawtuxet Valley Preservation and Historical Society. He is also a founding member of the board of directors of the Association of Rhode Island Authors (ARIA).

He has written six historical books in the Images of America series by Arcadia Publishing and this is his sixth book in the Gramma Larson Remembers series. He has also published; *A Bicycle Odyssey, Route 66 Today* and *Rhode Island Diners Today.*

In 2012 he was the premier member of the Rhode Island Historical Society to be in the new feature, Member Spotlight, of the RIHS quarterly magazine.

Ray was also named Citizen of the Year by the Rhode Island State Grange in 2015 for all of the work he has done in preserving local history, volunteering his time, and contributing to local historical societies.

Made in the
USA
Middletown, DE